Totus Tuus

A Consecration
to Jesus Through Mary with
Blessed John Paul II

By Fr. Brian McMaster

Our Sunday Visitor Publis
Our Sunday Visito
Huntington, Indiana

D1409860

Nihil Obstat
Msgr. Michael Heintz, Ph.D., *Censor Librorum*
Imprimatur
✠ Kevin C. Rhoades, Bishop of Fort Wayne-South Bend
September 7, 2012

The *Nihil Obstat* and *Imprimatur* are official declarations that a book is free from doctrinal or moral error. It is not implied that those who have granted the **Nihil Obstat** and *Imprimatur* agree with the contents, opinions, or statements expressed.

TABLE OF CONTENTS

INTRODUCTION

Totus Tuus — "Entirely Yours" — was the papal motto of Blessed John Paul the Great. The motto refers specifically to Mary and was taken from a daily Marian consecration prayer composed by Saint Louis de Montfort. For Blessed John Paul II these words expressed a loving entrustment to Mary — a total consecration — of all that he was so that he might be more fully conformed and consecrated to Jesus.

The purpose of *total consecration* is to deepen our relationship with God by entering into a loving communion with Mary that leads us to an intimate relationship with the Trinity and a radical conformity to Jesus Christ. The consecration asks that you surrender and give everything that is yours to Mary and thus to Jesus.

Why through Mary? Why not directly to Jesus? The goal of all true and genuine devotion to Mary is not only to lead us directly to Jesus but to do so in a more complete and total way. True devotion to Mary subtracts nothing from our due worship and adoration of Jesus Christ as God. Nor does it mitigate his saving action. Rather, our capacity to love Jesus in a singular way is magnified. From the cross, Jesus gave us Mary as our spiritual mother precisely so that we may benefit from her intercession for us as his beloved disciples. By going through Mary to Jesus, we "attach" ourselves in a familial way to her perfect fidelity and devotion. We actually increase and expand our capacity to be devoted to Jesus and the Blessed Trinity. The one who consecrates himself to Jesus through Mary will find himself going to Jesus *more directly* and more fully.

The more you give of yourself — the more generous you are — the more you will find that you have actually lost nothing, but rather have gained everything. God is never outdone in generosity. The new life of total consecration will lead you to greater holiness, peace of heart, love, virtue, happiness, and freedom.

Saint Louis de Montfort and True Devotion to Mary

Saint Louis Marie Grignon de Montfort was born in 1673 in the small town of Montfort-la-Canne in the Brittany region of France. He was ordained a priest in 1700. A zealous priest and charismatic preacher, Saint Louis served as an apostolic missionary and traveled from parish to parish in western France preaching missions, instructing the people, helping the poor, and giving retreats. It was said that never did a sinner resist conversion to Jesus and Mary after being touched by de Montfort with a rosary. His spiritual masterpiece is *True Devotion to Mary*. In this treatise, he explains how genuine devotion to Mary is the shortest and surest path to Jesus Christ and the Holy Trinity. He proposes a total consecration to Jesus through Mary as an adult form of renewing one's baptismal promises. Countless individuals of every vocation and walk of life have read *True Devotion to Mary* and given themselves in consecration to Jesus through Mary.

It may be helpful to summarize briefly some of the elements intrinsic to Saint Louis de Montfort's form of total consecration:

> **1. Christocentric.** The first fundamental truth that Saint Louis says is necessary for genuine Marian devotion is that it is directed to Jesus Christ. He explains, "If then we establish solid devotion to Our Blessed Lady it is only to establish more perfectly devotion to Jesus Christ" (*TD*, 62). Devotion to Mary, therefore, is never for its own end,

but must be pointed toward the final end of union with Jesus Christ.

2. Trinitarian. Through consecration to Jesus through Mary, we are enabled to give greater glory to God the Father. The Holy Spirit, likewise, is integral to a life of consecration. The Spirit, upon finding Mary, his receptive spouse, in a soul comes to it more readily with his grace and manifold gifts.

3. Rooted in the Mysteries of the Incarnation and Redemption. As the Eternal Wisdom of God took on flesh — that is, became incarnate in the womb of Mary and carried out our redemption by taking unto himself our humanity — so also a life of consecration logically follows along this same Marian path. As Saint Louis de Montfort writes in his work *Secret of Mary:* "If we would go up to God, and be united with Him, we must use the same means He used to come down to us to be made Man and to impart His graces to us. This means is a true devotion to our Blessed Lady" (23). Jesus becomes enlivened within us through Mary's presence in us and brings us to share in the divine life of the Trinity through our baptism and ongoing conversion.

4. Baptismal Renewal. Total consecration renews our baptismal identity in Christ as beloved sons and daughters of God. It is a way of responding to our baptismal call to holiness.

5. Total. Saint Louis instructs us that in a consecration that is total we give all that we are, including our body, our soul, our exterior goods, and our interior and spiritual goods. According to Saint Louis we become "slaves" of Mary and thus of Christ. We may at first be uncomfortable with this type of language, but essentially it means to belong totally to another and to hold nothing back. This *holy* *slavery* spoken of by Saint Louis de Montfort translates to John Paul II's concept of the *total gift of self.*

Blessed John Paul II

John Paul II's Marian spirituality, learned from Saint Louis de Montfort, not only enriched his own relationship with God, but through his saintly example and teaching also blessed the entire Church. In his memoirs of his fiftieth anniversary of priestly ordination, he shares about his discovery of Saint Louis de Montfort's *True Devotion to Mary* and reiterates the Christ-centered focus of Marian devotion:

> When I was in Cracow … a change took place in my understanding of devotion to the Mother of God. I was already convinced that Mary leads us to Christ, but at that time I began to realize also that Christ leads us to his Mother. At one point I began to question my devotion to Mary, believing that, if it became too great, it might end up compromising the supremacy of the worship owed to Christ. At that time, I was greatly helped by a book by Saint Louis Marie Grignon de Montfort entitled *Treatise of True Devotion to the Blessed Virgin.* There I found the answers to my questions. Yes, Mary does bring us closer to Christ; she does lead us to him, provided that we live her mystery in Christ … the essential theological truths which it contains are undeniable. The author is an outstanding theologian. His Mariological thought is rooted in the mystery of the Trinity and the truth of the Incarnation of the Word of God. And so thanks to Saint Louis, I began to discover the immense riches of Marian devotion from new perspectives. (*Gift and Mystery*, 28-29)

What Is Consecration?

The term "consecration" means that something or someone is made holy. Ultimately, God alone is holy. That anything else may be called holy means that God shares his life and holiness with it, thus separating it from the profane. Properly speaking, we do not "consecrate ourselves," but rather open ourselves like Mary to the gift of the Holy Spirit. We are incorporated into Christ by means of faith and baptism, and the life of charity takes root within us. In as much as we do speak of consecrating ourselves, we are saying "yes" in a cooperative way to entering into the consecration of Jesus when he prayed, "Sanctify them in the truth; your word is truth. As you sent me into the world, so I have sent them into the world. And for their sake I consecrate myself, that they also may be consecrated in truth" (Jn 17:17-19).

John Paul II used the word *consecration* and further developed its meaning by also using the word *entrustment*. For John Paul II, entrustment to Mary is the crowning expression and response to Jesus' mandate from the cross, "Behold, your mother." It is a response of love to the motherly love of Mary.

A New Approach with Blessed John Paul II

A growing number of Christians are seeking to consecrate themselves to Jesus through Mary, having heard of the powerful impact of such consecration in the lives of others, or having read that it was practiced by Blessed John Paul II. Many that attempt the preparation for total consecration by Saint Louis de Montfort, however, experience some difficulty with its style and language. It is, after all, about 300 years old, and written in a Baroque style that doesn't connect with our contemporary way of thinking. And yet the process of prayer that is outlined, the dynamic of giving oneself completely as a renewal of baptism, and the theological genius of *True Devotion* retain their value.

The purpose of this book is to take the best of Saint Louis de Montfort's *Preparation for Total Consecration* and freshen it with the thought and spirit of Blessed John Paul II, so that the modern reader and pray-er may enter more fully into a life of Marian consecration. We might say that the "personalism" of Blessed John Paul II polishes for the modern reader the gem that is already there in the total consecration put forth by Saint

Louis de Montfort. Characteristic to John Paul II's thought, personalism is a way of looking at reality from the perspective of the human person as its principal concern. For John Paul II, a person becomes the best version of himself when he lives in relationship with others — that is, in communion — and freely gives the *gift* of himself.

Consequently, this new approach to preparing for total consecration is attentive to the dynamic of relationship. The general outline and structure of Saint Louis's thirty-three-day preparation are retained, but each day's period of prayer is distinctly more contemplative and relational. There is a new arrangement of Scripture passages that is attentive to the dynamics of ongoing conversion and to developing a relationship with God and Mary. Many of the themes of Saint Louis are retained and the Trinitarian and Christocentric themes are highlighted and enhanced. Themes and writings of Blessed John Paul II, interspersed throughout the preparation, give a sense of being mentored by him. Through his own life of consecration, John Paul II has taught us how to love like Jesus and Mary.

Before You Get Started

You'll need to make some important preparations before you start. The first is commitment. Prayer requires commitment. The preparation for total consecration will require that you take fifteen to forty-five minutes a day for prayer for thirty-three consecutive days. Keep in mind that the consecration you are preparing for is for the rest of your life. And while there are times when you will be more faithful than others, it nonetheless requires a serious commitment to persevere in your devotion. Prayerfully consider, before you begin, whether you are ready to make this commitment. Be prudent, but also be generous.

Second, it is important to plan ahead of time when and where you will pray. Choose a time when you are mentally alert and a place where you won't be easily distracted. Remove all possible distractions such as phones and computers from the place where you pray. You might want to set up an area in your home — even just a corner of your room — that you can reserve solely for prayer, enhancing the environment with a crucifix, a statue or image of Mary, your Bible, and a candle. Use a comfortable chair, but one that helps you stay in an upright and attentive posture. When possible, you might want to pray in a church before the Blessed Sacrament.

Structure and Outline of the Preparation

This new version of the consecration follows the same outline as the thirty-three-day preparation written by Saint Louis de Montfort. The thirty-three days are divided into four distinct periods of prayer with different themes: twelve preliminary days, a week on the knowledge of self, a week on the knowledge of Mary, and a week on the knowledge of Jesus. The number thirty-three is itself an allusion to the thirty-three years of Christ's life. The symbolic number of days is a helpful reminder that the goal of consecration is to lead and direct us to Jesus Christ.

The purpose of the *Preliminary Days* is to immerse us in some of the fundamentals of the Christian life, and so dispose us for the more focused weeks on self, Mary, and Jesus. The period is referred to as preliminary because the days familiarize us with the foundations needed to receive the grace of communion that comes through praying the consecration. In Saint Louis's design, the preliminary days would be prayed the first time the preparation for consecration is prayed and are optional thereafter when renewing the consecration (which you are encouraged to do yearly). The *First Week* begins on Day 13, concludes on Day 19, and is focused on knowledge of self. The *Second Week* lasts from Day 20 through Day 26 and is dedicated to growing in knowledge of Mary. During this week, you will begin praying the Rosary in addition to the regular preparation prayers. The *Third Week* concludes the days of preparation from Day 27 to Day 33 and is focused on the knowledge of Jesus. The act of consecration is prayed on the next day following the preparation on what would be the thirty-fourth day.

How to Pray the Preparation for Total Consecration

The best way to look at each day of prayer is as a loving encounter that develops a cherished relationship. Avoid looking upon the prayer time as merely a series of exercises with multiple prayers to recite and passages to read. The goal, each day, is to open your heart to more contemplatively receive God's loving presence, to enter a loving communion with Mary, and to do so in such a way that it becomes a habituated way of being.

The following are the steps of prayer that you will take each day:

> **1. An Act of Presence.** The saints recommend beginning prayer with an *act of presence* that helps us to be aware of God's presence and focus our attention on him. We will use the Angelus as a way of becoming aware of the loving presence of the Trinity and Mary. The Angelus, a traditional prayer that commemorates the Annunciation, draws us into the receptivity of Mary, the "yes" of her heart. We "stand" with her and become aware of the love of the Father, the Holy Spirit overshadowing us, and the Son becoming present. Again, we shouldn't rush through this, but rather pray with a profound sense that Jesus is coming to be with us in Mary as at the Annunciation.

> **2. Prayer for the Light of the Holy Spirit.** Next, we pray for the Light of the Holy Spirit to guide our prayer. Saint Paul says, "For we do not know how to pray as we ought, but the Spirit himself intercedes for us with sighs too deep for words" (Rom 8:26). This step frees us from the tendency to judge our prayer for we call upon the Holy Spirit to direct us, trusting that he will guide our prayer where it's meant to go. Depending on the week, we will use the *Veni Creator Spiritus*, or the Litany of the Holy Spirit, as our

prayer for the Light of the Holy Spirit — the same prayers Saint Louis de Montfort recommends in his *Preparation*.

Don't rush through the prayer just to get through it, but rather expand your expectation that the Holy Spirit is in fact dwelling within you, stirring your heart, and conceiving the presence of Christ within you. When praying the *Veni Creator Spiritus*, linger on the phrase or word that gives you the greatest confidence in the Spirit's intercession. In praying the Litany to the Holy Spirit, be attentive to the Spirit gently but certainly penetrating your heart more deeply with each invocation that you pray. The Spirit's action is like water seeping into the soil.

3. Form Your Desire. Saint Augustine says that all prayer is desire. Forming your desire helps you to anticipate the grace that God already wants to give you and thus disposes you to be more ready and receptive to receive it. Each day of prayer includes a suggested desire. Form the desire in your own heart by softly repeating and assuming it as your own desire. Let the desire point and aim your heart toward the grace that God wants to give you. Keep repeating the desire until it's your own. Feel free to change the words so that the desire formed in your heart is *your* desire.

4. Contemplation. This is the heart of each day's prayer. Each contemplation includes a passage from Scripture and a reflection from either Blessed John Paul II or Saint Louis de Montfort. Start by reading the passages slowly and reflectively, expecting God to speak a word of love to you through them. Anticipate that the Holy Spirit will direct you to that word of love. Let yourself be drawn to the words or word where you feel the Lord drawing you, inviting you to stay and remain. Let yourself linger on these words, repeating them gently. Take time to meditate on the words and what their relevance is to you personally.

Having received the words of love and encounter into your heart, now speak to the Lord heart-to-heart about them. You may choose to speak to any or all the members of the Trinity. Speak to Mary as well. After speaking to the Trinity and Mary, take time to remain in silence with the presence of God's love in your heart. Be content to stay and rest. Move your will to simply receive God's love and Mary's love. Believe in faith that their love is being given to you.

5. Resolutions for Forming a Life of Marian Consecration. Following the contemplation, you will choose and make resolutions to help develop a life of Marian consecration. Total consecration isn't about getting to the end of the thirty-three days and hoping that something magically happens to change you. Rather, it is a gradual habituation of love and communion with Mary that opens your heart to the life of the Trinity. The resolution section offers a brief reflection to point you in the direction of forming a new way of life. It may be a motive for consecration suggested by Saint Louis de Montfort — allow it to stretch your desire. It may be an aspect of Marian consecration — resolve to form it as a habitual disposition.

The second week of preparation (Knowledge of Mary) aims to teach you how to pray the Rosary contemplatively, so that you may persevere in the practice of praying a daily Rosary as part of your new life of consecration. Each section also contains some suggested resolutions for the day. You may want to customize them to make them your own. Move your will to accept and choose them. Recall your resolutions throughout the day.

6. Close Your Time of Prayer. Close your prayer each day with either the Magnificat and Glory Be (the preliminary days), the Memorare (the first week), a prayer to Mary (the second week), or a prayer to Jesus and the Holy Spirit (the third week). Each of these devotional prayers will help bring a joyful and grateful conclusion to your time of prayer.

7. Journal. It is strongly recommended that you keep a journal during your preparation. You do not have to write a lot, but it would be helpful to note images, words, new discoveries, and felt sentiments that occurred in prayer. Be attentive to recording your thoughts, feelings, and desires. A daily record will help you be more keenly aware and discerning of the movement of the Holy Spirit.

Consecration: A New Way of Life Awaits You!

As you begin this preparation for consecration, take a moment to consider that God has already planned in his heart for you to enter this consecration, and Mary is welcoming you right now as you begin. The preparation for consecration will take you to a new level in your prayer life and, consequently, your relationship with God. It is meant to change your life. For some, the suggested methods of praying contemplatively may be new and challenging. Do not give in to worrying about how well you're praying or progressing. Simply trust, open your heart to love, and be generous.

Feel free to look ahead and read the introductions to each period, especially for the day of consecration. There are some instructions that require you to plan ahead of time.

Now, let us begin.

Totus Tuus ego sum et omnia mea tua sunt.
("I am totally yours, and all that I have is yours.")

THIRTY-THREE-DAY PREPARATION
FOR TOTAL CONSECRATION SCHEDULE

The preparation for total consecration lasts thirty-three days. On the thirty-fourth day, you will pray the act of consecration. Saint Louis de Montfort suggests making the act of consecration on a Marian feast day. Here is a table to guide you in choosing a consecration day and determining when to start the preparation.

Date to Start	Feast Day	Consecration Day
November 29	Mary, Mother of God	January 1
January 9	Our Lady of Lourdes	February 11
February 20	The Annunciation	March 25
March 26	Saint Louis de Montfort	April 28
April 10	Our Lady of Fátima	May 13
April 28	Visitation	May 31
May 25	Our Mother of Perpetual Help	June 27
June 13	Our Lady of Mount Carmel	July 16
July 13	The Assumption	August 15
July 20	Coronation of Mary	August 22
July 24	Our Lady of Czestochowa	August 26
August 6	Nativity of the Blessed Virgin Mary	September 8
August 10	Holy Name of Mary	September 12
August 13	Our Lady of Sorrows	September 15
September 4	Our Lady of the Rosary	October 7
September 19	Blessed John Paul II	October 22
October 19	Presentation of the Blessed Virgin Mary	November 21
November 5	Immaculate Conception	December 8
November 9	Our Lady of Guadalupe	December 12

ABBREVIATIONS AND REFERENCES

Saint Louis de Montfort:

SM	*Secret of Mary*
TD	*True Devotion to Mary* (St. Benedict Press, TAN Books, *True Devotion to Mary with Preparation for Total Consecration*, Saint Louis de Montfort)

Blessed John Paul II:

CL	*Christifideles Laici*
CTH	*Crossing the Threshold of Hope*
DM	*Dives in Misericordia*
DV	*Dominum et Vivificantem*
Gen. Aud.	General audience given on the date specified
EE	*Ecclesia de Eucharistia*
GM	*Gift and Mystery*
Homily	Homily given on the date specified
MR	*Redemptoris Missio*
NMI	*Novo Millennio Ineunte*
RH	*Redemptor Hominis*
RM	*Redemptoris Mater*
RP	*Reconciliatio et Paenitentia*
RVM	*Rosarium Virginis Mariae*
SD	*Salvifici Doloris*
TMA	*Tertio Millennio Adveniente*
VS	*Veritatis Splendor*

Other:

CCC	*Catechism of the Catholic Church*
LG	*Lumen Gentium* Dogmatic Constitution on the Church, Second Vatican Council
GS	*Gaudium et Spes* Pastoral Constitution on the Church in the Modern World, Second Vatican Council

THE PRELIMINARY DAYS

The Love of the Trinity and the Call to Repentance

The preliminary days begin with a focus on the Trinity and then move to explore themes of repentance. Marian consecration is ultimately meant to point us to a life of communion with the Father, Son, and Holy Spirit. By first centering our attention on the love of the Triune God, we are better prepared and motivated to repent from all obstacles to that communion and undergo heartfelt conversion. "We love, because he first loved us" (1 Jn 4:19). From the vantage point of God's love, we are moved to genuine repentance — to reform our lives, to detach ourselves from the spirit of the world, turn away from sin, and turn more fully to God. This is exactly how the grace of baptism unfolds in our lives.

Saint Louis de Montfort recommends that we regularly examine our conscience during this period. Such an examination should be done within the context of God's love. We desire to have a humble and genuine sorrow for our sins, but want to avoid excessive shame or any kind of self-hatred or self-loathing. Allow the examination of conscience to go deeper than usual.

Try to trace and understand what attachments and compulsions are underneath your sins.

The ninth day of the preparation will recommend the Sacrament of Reconciliation. You can do this on that day, one of the remaining preliminary days, or even into the first week if necessary. This is a tremendous opportunity to experience God's love, mercy, and healing. "Be not afraid," as Blessed John Paul II often reminded the world. If there are things that you've been afraid to bring to confession in the past, now is the time. You will receive the Sacrament of Reconciliation again at the end of the preparation, around the day of consecration.

Saint Louis further recommends that we become aware of how the spirit of the world affects us and draws us subtly away from God through the lures of money, status, success, material possessions, pleasure, and so forth. If you discover that any of these influences affect you in an inordinate way, begin to move your will away from them in order to more freely reorient yourself toward God.

Practicing self-denial through various forms of fasting, giving things up, and renouncement of your will are helpful practices during the preliminary days. Jesus said, "If any man would come after me, let him deny himself and take up his cross daily and follow me. For whoever would save his life will lose it; and whoever loses his life for my sake, he will save it" (Lk 9:23-24). The traditional fast is from food, but we can also fast from various forms of technology or from other luxuries, comforts, and pleasures. When you find yourself wanting the thing you've given up, let that serve as a reminder to turn to God who is our ultimate satisfaction and security.

Remember that your sacrifices are not for their own sake or to prove to yourself that you can do them, but rather they are for *his* sake. It may be helpful to give some consideration to these resolutions as you begin the preliminary days. The most fruitful resolutions are likely to be those that are moderate and yet firm.

PRAYERS TO BE USED DURING THE PRELIMINARY DAYS

Angelus

V. The angel of the Lord declared unto Mary.

R. And she conceived by the power of the Holy Spirit.

Hail Mary ...

V. Behold the handmaid of the Lord.

R. Be it done unto me according to your Word.

Hail Mary ...

V. And the Word was made flesh.

R. And dwelt among us.

Hail Mary ...

V. Pray for us, O Holy Mother of God.

R. That we may be made worthy of the promises of Christ.

Let us pray.

Pour forth, we beseech you, O Lord, your grace into our hearts, that we to whom the incarnation of Christ your Son was made known by the message of an angel, may by his Passion and Cross be brought to the glory of his resurrection; through the same Christ our Lord. Amen.

Veni Creator Spiritus

Come, O Creator Spirit blest!
And in our souls take up Thy rest;
Come with Thy grace and heavenly aid,
To fill the hearts which Thou hast made.

Great Paraclete! To Thee we cry,

O highest gift of God most high!
O font of life! O fire of love!
And sweet anointing from above.

Thou in Thy sevenfold gifts art known,
The finger of God's hand we own;
The promise of the Father, Thou!
Who dost the tongue with power endow.

Kindle our senses from above,
And make our hearts overflow with love;
With patience firm and virtue high
The weakness of our flesh supply.

Far from us drive the foe we dread,
And grant us Thy true peace instead;
So shall we not, with Thee for guide,
Turn from the path of life aside.

Oh, may Thy grace on us bestow
The Father and the Son to know,
And Thee, through endless times confessed,
Of both, the eternal Spirit blest.

All glory while the ages run
Be to the Father and the Son
Who rose from death; the same to Thee,
O Holy Spirit, eternally. Amen.

Magnificat

My soul proclaims the greatness of the Lord,
my spirit rejoices in God my Savior
for He has looked with favor on his lowly servant.

From this day all generations will call me blessed:
the Almighty has done great things for me,
and holy is his Name.

He has mercy on those who fear him
in every generation.

He has shown the strength of his arm,
he has scattered the proud in their conceit.

He has cast down the mighty from their thrones,
and has lifted up the lowly.

He has filled the hungry with good things,
and the rich He has sent away empty.

He has come to the help of his servant Israel
for he has remembered his promise of mercy,
the promise he made to our fathers,
to Abraham and his children for ever.

Glory Be

Glory be to the Father, and to the Son, and to the Holy
Spirit.
As it was in the beginning, is now, and ever shall be,
world without end. Amen.

The Trinity's Loving Plan in Mary

Begin Your Prayer

Pray the Angelus as an act of presence: Consider the Father's loving gaze upon you, Jesus becoming present to you in Mary, and the Holy Spirit overshadowing you.

Pray for the Light of the Holy Spirit: Pray the *Veni Creator Spiritus*, asking and trusting that the Holy Spirit guide, enrich, and inspire your time of prayer.

Form your desire: Gratitude for God's loving plan to share his life with you through Mary.

Contemplation

Read slowly and reflectively from Scripture:

> But when the time had fully come, God sent forth his Son, born of woman, born under the law, to redeem those who were under the law, so that we might receive adoption as sons. And because you are sons, God has sent the Spirit of his Son into our hearts, crying, "Abba! Father!" So through God you are no longer a slave but a son, and if a son then an heir. (Gal 4:4-7)

From the *Catechism of the Catholic Church*:

> By sending his only Son and the Spirit of Love in the fullness of time, God has revealed his innermost secret (cf. 1 Cor 2:7-16; Eph 3:9-12): God himself is an eternal exchange of love, Father, Son, and Holy Spirit, and he has destined us to share in that exchange. (221)

From Blessed John Paul II:

"When the fullness of time had come, God sent forth his Son, born of woman" (Gal 4:4). The fullness of time coincides with the mystery of the Incarnation of the Word, of the Son who is of one being with the Father, and with the mystery of the Redemption of the world. In this passage, Saint Paul emphasizes that the Son of God was born of woman, born under the Law, and came into the world in order to redeem all who were under the Law, so that they might receive adoption as sons and daughters. And he adds: "Because you are sons, God has sent the Spirit of his Son into our hearts, crying 'Abba! Father!'" His conclusion is truly comforting: "So through God you are no longer a slave but a son, and if a son then an heir" (Gal 4:6-7). Paul's presentation of the mystery of the Incarnation contains the revelation of the mystery of the Trinity and the continuation of the Son's mission in the mission of the Holy Spirit.

The Incarnation of the Son of God, his conception and birth, is the prerequisite for the sending of the Holy Spirit. This text of Saint Paul thus allows the fullness of the mystery of the Redemptive Incarnation to shine forth (*NMI*, 1).

[Mary] is the way that leads to Christ: indeed, she who "at the message of the angel received the Word of God in her heart and in her body" (*LG*, 53) shows us how to receive into our lives the Son come down from heaven, teaching us to make Jesus the center and the supreme "law" of our existence. (*Gen. Aud.*, January 10, 1996)

- *Return to the words and phrases to which you are most drawn by the Lord. Ponder them reflectively.*

- *Pray from your heart, conversing with the Father, Jesus, the Holy Spirit, and/or Mary.*

- *Pause and receive from God in silent prayer.*

Resolutions for Forming a Life of Marian Consecration

Genuine Marian consecration is directed to Jesus Christ, rooted in the Trinity, and is a perfect renewal of your baptism. Blessed John Paul II, reflecting on his own Marian devotion, said:

> At first it seemed to me that I should distance myself a bit from the Marian devotion of my childhood, in order to focus more on Christ. Thanks to Saint Louis [de] Montfort, I came to understand that true devotion to the Mother of God is actually Christocentric, indeed it is very profoundly rooted in the mystery of the Blessed Trinity, and the mysteries of the Incarnation and Redemption. And so, I rediscovered Marian piety, this time with a deeper understanding. (*CTH*, p. 213)

Suggested Resolutions for Today

- *As you begin your preparation for consecration, form a confident trust that Mary has already begun to intercede for you. Trust that she is leading you to Christ, and in Christ to the freedom of being a son or daughter of God.*

- *Begin to cultivate the habit of pausing throughout the day to become aware and attentive to Mary's presence with you.*

- *Consider how all the persons of the Trinity are laboring to give you love.*

Close Your Time of Prayer

With thanksgiving in your heart, pray with Mary the Magnificat and the Glory Be.

DAY 2

Jesus,
the Word Incarnate

Begin Your Prayer

Pray the Angelus as an act of presence: Consider the Father's loving gaze upon you, Jesus becoming present to you in Mary, and the Holy Spirit overshadowing you.

Pray for the Light of the Holy Spirit: Pray the *Veni Creator Spiritus*, asking and trusting that the Holy Spirit guide, enrich, and inspire your time of prayer.

Form your desire: Joyful anticipation of being led to a deeper relationship with Jesus through Mary.

Contemplation

Read slowly and reflectively from Scripture:

In the beginning was the Word, and the Word was with God, and the Word was God. He was in the beginning with God; all things were made through him, and without him was not anything made that was made. In him was life, and the life was the light of men. The light shines in the darkness, and the darkness has not overcome it.

There was a man sent from God, whose name was John. He came for testimony, to bear witness to the light, that all might believe through him. He was not the light, but came to bear witness to the light.

The true light that enlightens every man was coming into the world. He was in the world, and the world was made through him, yet the world knew him not. He came to his own home, and his own people received him not. But to all who received him, who believed in his name, he gave power to become children of God; who were born, not of blood nor of the will of the flesh nor of the will of man, but of God.

And the Word became flesh and dwelt among us, full of grace and truth; we have beheld his glory, glory as of the only Son from the Father. (John bore witness to him, and cried, "This was he of whom I said, 'He who comes after me ranks before me, for he was before me.'") And from his fulness have we all received, grace upon grace. For the law was given through Moses; grace and truth came through Jesus Christ. No one has ever seen God; the only Son, who is in the bosom of the Father, he has made him known. (Jn 1:1-18)

From Blessed John Paul II:

Christ is the foundation and center of history, he is its meaning and ultimate goal. It is in fact through him, the Word and image of the Father, that "all things were made" (Jn 1:3; cf. Col 1:15). His incarnation, culminating in the Paschal Mystery and the gift of the Spirit, is the pulsating heart of time, the mysterious hour in which the kingdom of God came to us (cf. Mk 1:15), indeed took root in our history, as the seed destined to become a great tree (cf. Mk 4:30-32). (*NMI*, 5)

It is Jesus in fact that you seek when you dream of happiness, he is waiting for you when nothing else you find satisfies you; he is the beauty to which you are so attracted; it is he who provokes you with that thirst for fullness that will not let you settle for compromise; it is he who urges you to shed the masks of a false life; it is he who reads in your hearts your most genuine choices, the choices that others try to stifle.

It is Jesus who stirs in you the desire to do something great with your lives, the will to follow an ideal, the refusal to allow yourselves to be ground down by mediocrity, the courage to commit yourselves humbly and patiently to improving yourselves and society, making the world more human and more fraternal. (*World Youth Day 2000 Prayer Vigil*, August 19, 2000)

- *Return to the words and phrases to which you are most drawn by the Lord. Ponder them reflectively.*
- *Pray from your heart, conversing with the Father, Jesus, the Holy Spirit, and/or Mary.*
- *Pause and receive from God in silent prayer.*

Resolutions for Forming a Life of Marian Consecration

The aim of Marian consecration is to lead one to a greater love, praise, and reverence of Jesus Christ. Saint Louis de Montfort speaks of this fundamental truth:

As all perfection consists in our being conformed, united and consecrated to Jesus it naturally follows that the most perfect of all devotions is that which conforms, unites, and consecrates us most completely to Jesus. Now of all God's creatures Mary is the most conformed to Jesus. It therefore follows that, of all devotions, devotion to her makes for the most effective consecration and conformity to him. The more one is consecrated to Mary, the more one is consecrated to Jesus. That is why perfect consecration to Jesus is but a perfect and complete consecration of oneself to the Blessed Virgin, which is the devotion I teach; or in other words, it is the perfect renewal of the vows and promises of holy baptism. (*TD*, 120)

Suggested Resolutions for Today

- *Consider the goal of Marian consecration: to lead you to a deeper relationship with Jesus Christ.*

- *Continue forming the habit of pausing throughout the day to become attentive to Mary's presence. Use these moments today to speak to Jesus with Mary beside you.*

Close Your Time of Prayer

With thanksgiving in your heart, pray with Mary the Magnificat and the Glory Be.

DAY 3

God,
the Father

Begin Your Prayer

Pray the Angelus as an act of presence: Consider the Father's loving gaze upon you, Jesus becoming present to you in Mary, and the Holy Spirit overshadowing you.

Pray for the Light of the Holy Spirit: Pray the *Veni Creator Spiritus*, asking and trusting that the Holy Spirit guide, enrich, and inspire your time of prayer.

Form your desire: A new sense of love and awe of God your Father.

Contemplation

Read slowly and reflectively from Scripture:

> Jesus said to him, "I am the way, and the truth, and the life; no one comes to the Father, but by me. If you had known me, you would have known my Father also; henceforth you know him and have seen him." Philip said to him, "Lord, show us the Father, and we shall be satisfied." Jesus said to him, "Have I been with you so long, and yet you do not know me, Philip? He who has seen me has seen the Father; how can you say, 'Show us the Father'? Do you not believe that I am in the Father and the Father in me? The words that I say to you I do not speak on my own authority; but the Father who dwells in me does his works. Believe me that I am in the Father and the Father in me;

or else believe me for the sake of the works themselves. (Jn 14:6-11)

From Blessed John Paul II:

Above all, Jesus stands in an absolutely unique relationship to the divine fatherhood, revealing himself as "son" and offering himself as the one way to reach the Father. To Philip, who asked, "show us the Father, and we shall be satisfied," he replies that knowing him means knowing the Father, because the Father works through him. Therefore those who want to meet the Father must believe in the Son: through him God does not merely assure us of his providential fatherly care, but communicates his own life, making us "sons in the Son."

This is what the apostle John emphasizes with a deep sense of gratitude: "See what love the Father has given us, that we should be called children of God; and so we are" (1 Jn 3:1). (*Gen. Aud.*, January 13, 1999)

- *Return to the words and phrases to which you are most drawn by the Lord. Ponder them reflectively.*

- *Pray from your heart, conversing with the Father, Jesus, the Holy Spirit, and/or Mary.*

- *Pause and receive from God in some time of silent prayer.*

Resolutions for Forming a Life of Marian Consecration

Jesus reveals God the Father to us, and through the Holy Spirit we are made beloved sons and daughters in Christ. Blessed John Paul II notes, "Mother of the Son, Mary is the 'beloved daughter of the Father' in a unique way" (*Gen. Aud.*, January 10, 1996). Leading us to Christ, Marian consecration opens a wider horizon for us to appreciate our own identity as children of God.

Suggested Resolutions for Today

- *Take a few moments to reflect on what Jesus wants to reveal to you about your heavenly Father.*

- *Periodically throughout the day, turn in prayer to the Father. With a sense of Jesus and Mary being with you, joyfully receive the love of the Father for you as his beloved son or daughter.*

Close Your Time of Prayer

With thanksgiving in your heart, pray with Mary the Magnificat and the Glory Be.

DAY 4

The Holy Spirit

Begin Your Prayer

Pray the Angelus as an act of presence: Consider the Father's loving gaze upon you, Jesus becoming present to you in Mary, and the Holy Spirit overshadowing you.

Pray for the Light of the Holy Spirit: Pray the *Veni Creator Spiritus,* asking and trusting that the Holy Spirit guide, enrich, and inspire your time of prayer.

Form your desire: An opening of your heart in faith to the gift of the Holy Spirit.

Contemplation

Read slowly and reflectively from Scripture:

"If you love me, you will keep my commandments. And I will ask the Father, and he will give you another Counselor, to be with you for ever, even the Spirit of truth, whom the world cannot receive, because it neither sees him nor knows him; you know him, for he dwells with you, and will be in you.

"I will not leave you desolate; I will come to you. Yet a little while, and the world will see me no more, but you will see me; because I live, you will live also. In that day you will know that I am in my Father, and you in me, and I in you. He who has my commandments and keeps them, he it is who loves me; and he who loves me will be loved by my Father, and I will love him and manifest myself to him." (Jn 14:15-21)

From Blessed John Paul II:

In his intimate life, God "is love" (cf. 1 Jn 4:8,16) the essential love shared by the three divine Persons: personal love is the Holy Spirit as the Spirit of the Father and the Son. Therefore he "searches even the depths of God" (cf. 1 Cor 2:10), as uncreated Love-Gift.

It can be said that in the Holy Spirit the intimate life of the Triune God becomes totally gift, an exchange of mutual love between the divine Persons and that through the Holy Spirit God exists in the mode of gift. It is the Holy Spirit who is the personal expression of this self-giving, of this being-love. He is Person-Love. He is Person-Gift. (*DV*, 10)

- *Return to the words and phrases to which you are most drawn by the Lord. Ponder them reflectively.*

- *Pray from your heart, conversing with the Father, Jesus, the Holy Spirit, and/or Mary.*

- *Pause and receive from God in some time of silent prayer.*

Resolutions for Forming a Life of Marian Consecration

In his encyclical letter on the Holy Spirit, Blessed John Paul II explores the nature of faith while commenting on Mary's obedience and openness, saying, "And faith, in its deepest essence, is the openness of the human heart to the gift: to God's self-communication in the Holy Spirit" (*DV*, 51). Marian consecration aims at increasing our own receptivity to God's gift in the Holy Spirit.

Suggested Resolutions for Today

- *Consider Mary's openness and docility to the Holy Spirit. Continue to be aware of her presence with you throughout the day. Allow her to draw you into her faith.*

- *Periodically throughout the day, turn in prayer to the Holy Spirit. With Mary beside you, seek to make her receptivity your own and consciously choose to open your heart to God's gift, his loving presence in the Holy Spirit.*

Close Your Time of Prayer

With thanksgiving in your heart, pray with Mary the Magnificat and the Glory Be.

DAY 5

The Spirit of the World

Begin Your Prayer

Pray the Angelus as an act of presence: Consider the Father's loving gaze upon you, Jesus becoming present to you in Mary, and the Holy Spirit overshadowing you.

Pray for the Light of the Holy Spirit: Pray the *Veni Creator Spiritus*, asking and trusting that the Holy Spirit guide, enrich, and inspire your time of prayer.

Form your desire: For a new freedom and determination to turn from pride and the insistence of worldly enticements to a fresh preference for the things of God.

Contemplation

Read slowly and reflectively from Scripture:

> Do not love the world or the things in the world. If any one loves the world, love for the Father is not in him. For all that is in the world, the lust of the flesh and the lust of the eyes and the pride of life, is not of the Father but is of the world. And the world passes away, and the lust of it; but he who does the will of God abides for ever. (1 Jn 2:15-17)

> I appeal to you therefore, brethren, by the mercies of God, to present your bodies as a living sacrifice, holy and acceptable to God, which is your spiritual worship. Do not be conformed to this world but be transformed by the renewal of your mind, that you may prove what is the will of God, what is good and acceptable and perfect. (Rom 12:1-2)

From Blessed John Paul II:

Listen to the voice of Jesus in the depths of your hearts! His words tell you who you are as Christians. They tell you what you must do to remain in His love. But Jesus offers one thing, and the "spirit of the world" offers another. ... The "spirit of the world" *offers many false illusions and parodies of happiness.* There is perhaps no darkness deeper than the darkness that enters young people's souls when false prophets extinguish in them the light of faith and hope and love. The greatest deception, and the deepest source of unhappiness, is *the illusion of finding life by excluding God,* of finding freedom by excluding moral truths and personal responsibility. (*Homily, World Youth Day,* Toronto, July 28, 2002)

From Saint Louis de Montfort:

The first part of the preparation should be employed in casting off the spirit of the world which is contrary to that of Jesus Christ. The spirit of the world consists essentially in the denial of the supreme dominion of God; a denial which is manifested in practice by sin and disobedience; thus it is principally opposed to the spirit of Christ, which is also that of Mary. It manifests itself by the concupiscence of the flesh, by the concupiscence of the eyes and by the pride of life; by disobedience to God's laws and the abuse of created things.

Its works are, first, sin in all its forms; and then all else by which the devil leads to sin; works which bring error and darkness to the mind, and seduction and corruption to the will. Its pomps are the splendor and the charms employed by the devil to render sin alluring in persons, places and things. (*Preparation for Consecration*)

- *Return to the words and phrases to which you are most drawn by the Lord. Ponder them reflectively.*

- *Pray from your heart, conversing with the Father, Jesus, the Holy Spirit, and/or Mary.*
- *Pause and receive from God in some time of silent prayer.*

Resolutions for Forming a Life of Marian Consecration

In the previous four days of preparation, you have seen that the aim of consecration is to draw you into a more loving relationship of communion with the Blessed Trinity — to receive God's love in a new and deeper way and to be moved to love Him in return. Mary helps you to turn to God in love and facilitates a greater freedom in letting go of attachments to created things. During these preliminary days of preparation it is important to identify where the spirit of the world is influencing your life, priorities, and choices. The resolutions you make in these days are critical in disposing you to more freely choose and receive the loving relationship God desires to give you.

Suggested Resolutions for Today

- *Examine your life and notice any influence of the spirit of the world. Ask Mary to help you let go of any inordinate or unhealthy attachments you may have.*

- *As Blessed John Paul II recommended, "listen to the voice of Jesus" in the depth of your heart so that you may know who you are as a Christian and what you must do to remain in his love.*

- *Consider fasting or giving something up today, in the coming days, or even for the remainder of the preliminary days.*

Close Your Time of Prayer

With thanksgiving in your heart, pray with Mary the Magnificat and the Glory Be.

DAY 6

The Beatitudes

Begin Your Prayer

Pray the Angelus as an act of presence: Consider the Father's loving gaze upon you, Jesus becoming present to you in Mary, and the Holy Spirit overshadowing you.

Pray for the Light of the Holy Spirit: Pray the *Veni Creator Spiritus*, asking and trusting that the Holy Spirit guide, enrich, and inspire your time of prayer.

Form your desire: For an intensified love for Jesus who became poor for your sake so that you may desire and choose a greater poverty of spirit.

Contemplation

Read slowly and reflectively from Scripture:

Seeing the crowds, he went up on the mountain, and when he sat down his disciples came to him. And he opened his mouth and taught them, saying: "Blessed are the poor in spirit, for theirs is the kingdom of heaven. Blessed are those who mourn, for they shall be comforted. Blessed are the meek, for they shall inherit the earth. Blessed are those who hunger and thirst for righteousness, for they shall be satisfied. Blessed are the merciful, for they shall obtain mercy. Blessed are the pure in heart, for they shall see God. Blessed are the peacemakers, for they shall be called sons of God. Blessed are those who are persecuted for righteousness' sake, for theirs is the kingdom of heaven. Blessed are you when men revile you and persecute you and utter all kinds of evil against you falsely on my account. Rejoice and be glad, for your reward is great in heaven, for so men persecuted the prophets who were before you." (Mt 5:1-12)

From Blessed John Paul II:

"Blessed are you!" he says, "all you who are poor in spirit, gentle and merciful, you who mourn, who care for what is right, who are pure in heart, who make peace, you who are persecuted! Blessed are you!" But the words of Jesus may seem strange. It is strange that Jesus exalts those whom the world generally regards as weak. He says to them, "Blessed are you who seem to be losers, because you are the true winners: the kingdom of heaven is yours!" Spoken by him who is "gentle and humble in heart" (Mt 11:29), these words present a challenge which demands a deep and abiding *metanoia* [conversion] of the spirit, a great change of heart....

To put your faith in Jesus means choosing to believe what he says, no matter how strange it may seem, and choosing to reject the claims of evil, no matter how sensible or attractive they may seem.

In the end, Jesus does not merely speak the Beatitudes. He lives the Beatitudes. He is the Beatitudes. Looking at him you will see what it means to be poor in spirit, gentle and merciful, to mourn, to care for what is right, to be pure in heart, to make peace, to be persecuted.

This is why he has the right to say, "Come, follow me!" He does not say simply, "Do what I say." He says, "Come, follow me!" (*Homily, Israel, Korazim, Mount of the Beatitudes*, March 24, 2000)

- *Return to the words and phrases to which you are most drawn by the Lord. Ponder them reflectively.*

- *Pray from your heart, conversing with the Father, Jesus, the Holy Spirit, and/or Mary.*

- *Pause and receive from God in some time of silent prayer.*

Resolutions for Forming a Life of Marian Consecration

Saint Louis speaks of various *motives* for Marian consecration — reasons that impel us to pursue this new way of life. One such motive is that Marian consecration gives us the privilege of devoting and offering all that we are to the service of God. Allow this motive to so move your heart and begin to practice the daily offering of your entire life — those areas of your life where you fear that you lack or are not enough.

> This devotion makes us give to Jesus and Mary, without reserve, all our thoughts, words, actions and sufferings, every moment of our life, in such wise that whether we wake or sleep, whether we eat or drink, whether we do great actions or very little ones, it is always true to say that whatever we do, even without thinking of it, is, by virtue of our offering — at least if it has not been intentionally retracted — done for Jesus and Mary. What a consolation this is! (*TD*, 135-136)

Suggested Resolutions for Today

- *With a sense of Mary beside you, begin to form the practice of briefly offering your thoughts, actions, sufferings, sleep, and every waking moment of your life to God.*

- *Move your heart to accept the consolation that your littleness, too, may be offered to Jesus through Mary.*

- *Become aware of where you are poor — your weaknesses, imperfections, your need for God's mercy and consolation. Allow these areas in your life to become places where in humble dependence you open yourself to receive God's compassion and saving love for you.*

Close Your Time of Prayer

With thanksgiving in your heart, pray with Mary the Magnificat and the Glory Be.

DAY 7

Prayer

Begin Your Prayer

Pray the Angelus as an act of presence: Consider the Father's loving gaze upon you, Jesus becoming present to you in Mary, and the Holy Spirit overshadowing you.

Pray for the Light of the Holy Spirit: Pray the *Veni Creator Spiritus*, asking and trusting that the Holy Spirit guide, enrich, and inspire your time of prayer.

Form your desire: To experience God's delight in you as you come to prayer.

Contemplation

Read slowly and reflectively from Scripture:

"And when you pray, you must not be like the hypocrites; for they love to stand and pray in the synagogues and at the street corners, that they may be seen by men. Truly, I say to you, they have received their reward. But when you pray, go into your room and shut the door and pray to your Father who is in secret; and your Father who sees in secret will reward you.

"And in praying do not heap up empty phrases as the Gentiles do; for they think that they will be heard for their many words. Do not be like them, for your Father knows what you need before you ask him. Pray then like this:

Our Father who art in heaven,
hallowed be thy name.
Thy kingdom come.
Thy will be done,

on earth as it is in heaven.
Give us this day our daily bread;
and forgive us our trespasses,
as we forgive those who trespass against us;
and lead us not into temptation,
but deliver us from evil." (Mt 6:5-13)

From Blessed John Paul II:

We cannot come to the fullness of contemplation of the
Lord's face by our own efforts alone, but by allowing grace
to take us by the hand. Only the experience of silence
and prayer offers the proper setting for the growth and
development of a true, faithful and consistent knowledge
of that mystery which finds its culminating expression in
the solemn proclamation by the Evangelist Saint John:
"And the Word became flesh and dwelt among us, full of
grace and truth; we have beheld his glory, glory as of the
only Son from the Father" (1:14). (*NMI*, 20)

- *Return to the words and phrases to which you are most drawn by the Lord. Ponder them reflectively.*

- *Pray from your heart, conversing with the Father, Jesus, the Holy Spirit, and/or Mary.*

- *Pause and receive from God in some time of silent prayer.*

Resolutions for Forming a Life of Marian Consecration

To form a life of Marian consecration means to form a life of
prayer. Mary teaches us a tenderness in prayer, how to contemplate the face of Jesus in love. This helps us to develop beyond
the beginnings of prayer — when we are perhaps concerned
more with "saying" our prayers — and moves us toward a
prayer of loving conversation, contemplative beholding, abiding in silence, and an exchange of the heart. Prayer is a gift, and
we should not be discouraged by any felt lack of proficiency at

prayer. We humbly turn to Jesus and ask him to teach us to pray as Blessed John Paul II recommends:

> We have to learn to pray: as it were learning this art ever anew from the lips of the Divine Master himself, like the first disciples: "Lord, teach us to pray!" (Lk 11:1). Prayer develops that conversation with Christ which makes us his intimate friends: "Abide in me and I in you" (Jn 15:4). (*NMI*, 32)

Suggested Resolutions for Today

- *Recommit yourself to the priority of prayer. Humbly speak to Jesus and Mary about any concerns you may have about your prayer life.*

- *Examine how your prayer time for the consecration is going. Do you need to make any adjustments?*

- *Be more attentive to the dynamic of silence in your prayer.*

Close Your Time of Prayer

With thanksgiving in your heart, pray with Mary the Magnificat and the Glory Be.

Trust in
Divine Providence

Begin Your Prayer

Pray the Angelus as an act of presence: Consider the Father's loving gaze upon you, Jesus becoming present to you in Mary, and the Holy Spirit overshadowing you.

Pray for the Light of the Holy Spirit: Pray the *Veni Creator Spiritus*, asking and trusting that the Holy Spirit guide, enrich, and inspire your time of prayer.

Form your desire: To feel peace at the Lord's command not to worry, and to find courage to reorient your life toward him.

Contemplation

Read slowly and reflectively from Scripture:

[Jesus] said to his disciples, "Therefore I tell you, do not be anxious about your life, what you shall eat, nor about your body, what you shall put on. For life is more than food, and the body more than clothing. Consider the ravens: they neither sow nor reap, they have neither storehouse nor barn, and yet God feeds them. Of how much more value are you than the birds! And which of you by being anxious can add a cubit to his span of life? If then you are not able to do as small a thing as that, why are you anxious about the rest? Consider the lilies, how they grow; they neither toil nor spin; yet I tell you, even Solomon in all his glory was not arrayed like one of these. But if God so clothes the grass which is alive in the field today and tomorrow is thrown into the oven, how much more will he clothe you, O men of little faith! And do not seek what you are to eat and what you are to drink, nor be of anxious mind. For all the nations of the world seek these things; and your Father knows that you need them. Instead, seek his kingdom, and these things shall be yours as well.

"Fear not, little flock, for it is your Father's good pleasure to give you the kingdom. Sell your possessions, and give alms; provide yourselves with purses that do not grow old, with a treasure in the heavens that does not fail, where no thief approaches and no moth destroys. For where your treasure is, there will your heart be also." (Lk 12:22-34)

From Blessed John Paul II:

To deny oneself is to give up one's own plans that are often small and petty in order to accept God's plan. This is the path of conversion, something indispensable in a Christian life, and that led Saint Paul to say, "it is no longer I who live, but Christ who lives in me" (Gal 2:20).

Jesus does not ask us to give up living, but to accept a newness and a fullness of life that only He can give. The human being has a deep-rooted tendency to "think only of self," to regard one's own person as the center of interest and to see oneself as the standard against which to gauge everything. One who chooses to follow Christ, on the other hand, avoids being wrapped up in himself and does not evaluate things according to self-interest. He looks on life in terms of gift and gratuitousness, not in terms of conquest and possession. Life in its fullness is only lived in self-giving, and that is the fruit of the grace of Christ: an existence that is free and in communion with God and neighbor (cf. *Gaudium et spes*, 24).

If to live as a follower of the Lord becomes the highest value, then all other values are given their rightful rank and importance. Whoever depends solely on worldly goods will end up by losing, even though there might seem to be an appearance of success. Death will find that person with an abundance of possessions but having lived a wasted life (cf. Lk 12:13-21). Therefore, the choice is between being and having, between a full life and an empty existence, between truth and falsehood. (*Message for World Youth Day XVI*, 2001)

- *Return to the words and phrases to which you are most drawn by the Lord. Ponder them reflectively.*
- *Pray from your heart, conversing with the Father, Jesus, the Holy Spirit, and/or Mary.*
- *Pause and receive from God in some time of silent prayer.*

Resolutions for Forming a Life of Marian Consecration

When we abide with Mary, we learn to trust in divine providence — God's loving plan. We enter into her fiat: "Let it be to me according to your word" (Lk 1:38). Mary fosters in us an interior freedom to trust God and not worry about making things work out our own way. Submitting to Mary will direct us to submission to God and a trustful abandonment to divine providence. Saint Louis de Montfort suggests this motive for Marian consecration: that we imitate Jesus in his own humble submission to Mary. God in his infinite wisdom came as a small child, submitted to the care of Mary, his mother, and waited for thirty years to begin his public ministry.

> He gave more glory to God his Father during all that time of submission to and dependence on our Blessed Lady than he would have given him if he had employed those thirty years in working miracles, in preaching to the whole world and in converting all men — all of which he would have done, could he have thereby contributed more to

God's glory. Oh, how highly we glorify God when, after the example of Jesus, we submit ourselves to Mary! (*TD*, 139)

Suggested Resolutions for Today

- *Identify areas of worry in your life. Place these anxieties into the hands of Mary. Be attentive to whether any of these areas point to unhealthy or worldly attachments.*

- *Consider the hopes and plans that you have for your life. With trust in your heart, entrust them in loving submission to Mary.*

Close Your Time of Prayer

With thanksgiving in your heart, pray with Mary the Magnificat and the Glory Be.

DAY 9

Acknowledging Sin

Begin Your Prayer

Pray the Angelus as an act of presence: Consider the Father's loving gaze upon you, Jesus becoming present to you in Mary, and the Holy Spirit overshadowing you.

Pray for the Light of the Holy Spirit: Pray the *Veni Creator Spiritus*, asking and trusting that the Holy Spirit guide, enrich, and inspire your time of prayer.

Form your desire: To feel a profound sorrow for your sins that urges you to acknowledge your sinfulness before God.

Contemplation

Read slowly and reflectively from Scripture:

> This is the message we have heard from him and proclaim to you, that God is light and in him is no darkness at all. If we say we have fellowship with him while we walk in darkness, we lie and do not live according to the truth; but if we walk in the light, as he is in the light, we have fellowship with one another, and the blood of Jesus his Son cleanses us from all sin.
>
> If we say we have no sin, we deceive ourselves, and the truth is not in us. If we confess our sins, he is faithful and just, and will forgive our sins and cleanse us from all unrighteousness. If we say we have not sinned, we make him a liar, and his word is not in us. (1 Jn 1:5-10)

From Blessed John Paul II:

> In the words of Saint John the Apostle, "If we say we have no sin, we deceive ourselves, and the truth is not in us. If

we confess our sins, he is faithful and just and will forgive our sins"(1 Jn 1:8-9)....

To acknowledge one's sin, indeed penetrating still more deeply into the consideration of one's own personhood to recognize oneself as being a sinner, capable of sin and inclined to commit sin, is the essential first step in returning to God. For example, this is the experience of David, who, "having done what is evil in the eyes of the Lord" and having been rebuked by the prophet Nathan (cf. 2 Sm 11-12), exclaims: "For I know my transgressions, and my sin is ever before me. Against you, you alone, have I sinned and done what is evil in your sight."(cf. Ps 51:3-4)

Similarly, Jesus himself puts the following significant words on the lips and in the heart of the prodigal son: "Father, I have sinned against heaven and before you" (Lk 15:18,21). In effect, to become reconciled with God presupposes and includes detaching oneself consciously and with determination from the sin into which one has fallen. It presupposes and includes, therefore, doing penance in the fullest sense of the term: repenting, showing this repentance, adopting a real attitude of repentance — which is the attitude of the person who starts out on the road of return to the Father. This is a general law and one which each individual must follow in his or her particular situation. (*RP*, 13)

- *Return to the words and phrases to which you are most drawn by the Lord. Ponder them reflectively.*

- *Pray from your heart, conversing with the Father, Jesus, the Holy Spirit, and/or Mary.*

- *Pause and receive from God in some time of silent prayer.*

Resolutions for Forming a Life of Marian Consecration

Blessed John Paul II encourages us to form a real attitude of repentance. To enter into Marian consecration means that we form the desire to be holy as God is holy (cf. Mt 5:48). As we continue in these preliminary days of preparation, we want to move our hearts to a sincere and determined repentance that seeks to remove our attachments to sin and to confidently turn to the Father and receive his loving mercy.

Suggested Resolutions for Today

- *While continuing to form your habit of offering everything to Mary, now offer to her the sorrow you have for your sin. Sense her loving acceptance of you and her desire to guide you to the mercy of her son.*

- *Resolve today to set out "on the road of return to the Father." Consider what this will mean for you.*

- *Examine your conscience and plan to receive the Sacrament of Reconciliation, either today or in one of the remaining preliminary days.*

Close Your Time of Prayer

With thanksgiving in your heart, pray with Mary the Magnificat and the Glory Be.

DAY 10

Mercy

Begin Your Prayer

Pray the Angelus as an act of presence: Consider the Father's loving gaze upon you, Jesus becoming present to you in Mary, and the Holy Spirit overshadowing you.

Pray for the Light of the Holy Spirit: Pray the *Veni Creator Spiritus*, asking and trusting that the Holy Spirit guide, enrich, and inspire your time of prayer.

Form your desire: To experience the cherishing love of God your Father and to feel healing in your heart through his merciful embrace.

Contemplation

Read slowly and reflectively from Scripture:

> And he said, "There was a man who had two sons; and the younger of them said to his father, 'Father, give me the share of property that falls to me.' And he divided his living between them. Not many days later, the younger son gathered all he had and took his journey into a far country, and there he squandered his property in loose living. And when he had spent everything, a great famine arose in that country, and he began to be in want. So he went and joined himself to one of the citizens of that country, who sent him into his fields to feed swine. And he would gladly have fed on the pods that the swine ate; and no one gave him anything. But when he came to himself he said, 'How many of my father's hired servants have bread enough and to spare, but I perish here with hunger! I will arise and go to my father, and I will say to

him, "Father, I have sinned against heaven and before you; I am no longer worthy to be called your son; treat me as one of your hired servants."'And he arose and came to his father. But while he was yet at a distance, his father saw him and had compassion, and ran and embraced him and kissed him. And the son said to him, 'Father, I have sinned against heaven and before you; I am no longer worthy to be called your son.' But the father said to his servants, 'Bring quickly the best robe, and put it on him; and put a ring on his hand, and shoes on his feet; and bring the fatted calf and kill it, and let us eat and make merry; for this my son was dead, and is alive again; he was lost, and is found.' And they began to make merry.

"Now his elder son was in the field; and as he came and drew near to the house, he heard music and dancing. And he called one of the servants and asked what this meant. And he said to him, 'Your brother has come, and your father has killed the fatted calf, because he has received him safe and sound.' But he was angry and refused to go in. His father came out and entreated him, but he answered his father, 'Behold, these many years I have served you, and I never disobeyed your command; yet you never gave me a kid, that I might make merry with my friends. But when this son of yours came, who has devoured your living with harlots, you killed for him the fatted calf!' And he said to him, 'Son, you are always with me, and all that is mine is yours. It was fitting to make merry and be glad, for this your brother was dead, and is alive; he was lost, and is found.'" (Lk 15:11-32)

From Blessed John Paul II:

Mercy — as Christ has presented it in the parable of the prodigal son — has the interior form of the love that in the New Testament is called agape. This love is able to reach down to every prodigal son, to every human misery, and above all to every form of moral misery, to sin. When this happens, the person who is the object of mercy does not feel humiliated, but rather found again and "restored to value."

The father first and foremost expresses to him his joy that he has been "found again" and that he has "returned to life." This joy indicates a good that has remained intact: even if he is a prodigal, a son does not cease to be truly his father's son; it also indicates a good that has been found again, which in the case of the prodigal son was his return to the truth about himself. (*DM*, 6)

- *Return to the words and phrases to which you are most drawn by the Lord. Ponder them reflectively.*

- *Pray from your heart, conversing with the Father, Jesus, the Holy Spirit, and/or Mary.*

- *Pause and receive from God in some time of silent prayer.*

Resolutions for Forming a Life of Marian Consecration

In receiving God's mercy we rediscover that "God is love" (1 Jn 4:8), and he reveals to us anew our dignity as beloved sons and daughters. Another motive Saint Louis de Montfort gives for Marian consecration is interior freedom by which we learn to relate to God more from love and less from fear.

This practice of devotion gives to those who make use of it faithfully a great interior liberty, which is the liberty of the children of God (Rom 8:21). Since, by this devotion, we make ourselves slaves of Jesus Christ and consecrate ourselves entirely to him in this capacity, our good Master, in recompense for the loving captivity in which we put ourselves, (1) takes from the soul all scruple and servile fear, which are capable only of cramping, imprisoning or confusing it; (2) he enlarges the heart with firm confidence in God, making it look upon him as a Father; and (3) he inspires us with a tender and filial love. (*TD*, 169)

Suggested Resolutions for Today

- *Ask Mary to help you receive God's love and mercy, especially in the areas where you experience the greatest misery, doubt, or weakness.*

- *Consider your own motives for serving God, whether they are from love or from fear. Learn from Mary the interior freedom to see God as a loving Father, and to thus serve him in love and not from fear.*

- *Let Mary calm the voice of the elder son in you that shuns or disbelieves — whether from shame, pride, or whatever reason — the mercy that God wants to give you.*

Close Your Time of Prayer

With thanksgiving in your heart, pray with Mary the Magnificat and the Glory Be.

DAY 11

God's Will

Begin Your Prayer

Pray the Angelus as an act of presence: Consider the Father's loving gaze upon you, Jesus becoming present to you in Mary, and the Holy Spirit overshadowing you.

Pray for the Light of the Holy Spirit: Pray the *Veni Creator Spiritus*, asking and trusting that the Holy Spirit guide, enrich, and inspire your time of prayer.

Form your desire: To experience a readiness and desire to seek God's will above all else.

Contemplation

Read slowly and reflectively from Scripture:

"Not every one who says to me, 'Lord, Lord,' shall enter the kingdom of heaven, but he who does the will of my Father who is in heaven. On that day many will say to me, 'Lord, Lord, did we not prophesy in your name, and cast out demons in your name, and do many mighty works in your name?' And then will I declare to them, 'I never knew you; depart from me, you evildoers.'" (Mt 7:21-23)

From Blessed John Paul II:

The words: "Let it be to me according to your word" (Lk 1:38), show in her who declared herself handmaid of the Lord, a total obedience to God's will. . . . By conforming to the divine will, Mary anticipates and makes her own the attitude of Christ....

Mary's docility likewise announces and prefigures that expressed by Jesus in the course of his public life until Calvary. Christ would say: "My food is to do the will of him who sent me, and to accomplish his work" (Jn 4:34). On these same lines, Mary makes the Father's will the inspiring principle of her whole life, seeking in it the necessary strength to fulfill the mission entrusted to her.

If at the moment of the Annunciation, Mary does not yet know of the sacrifice which will mark Christ's mission, Simeon's prophecy will enable her to glimpse her Son's tragic destiny (cf. Lk 3:34-35). The Virgin will be associated with him in intimate sharing. With her total obedience to God's will, Mary is ready to live all that divine love may plan for her life, even to the "sword" that will pierce her soul. (*Gen. Aud.* September 11, 1996)

- *Return to the words and phrases to which you are most drawn by the Lord. Ponder them reflectively.*

- *Pray from your heart, conversing with the Father, Jesus, the Holy Spirit, and/or Mary.*

- *Pause and receive from God in some time of silent prayer.*

Resolutions for Forming a Life of Marian Consecration

Giving ourselves more fully to Mary allows us to enter more fully into the pure gift of her heart and be formed by her sincere obedience of love. Often our motivations are not fully sincere or pure, but mixed. This may be so even though we're trying to do something to please God. Saint Louis de Montfort offers as another motive for consecration that *Mary purifies our good works and embellishes them.*

As by this practice we give to Our Lord, by his mother's hands, all our good works, that good Mother purifies them [and] embellishes them.... She purifies them of all the stain of self-love, and of that imperceptible attachment to created things which slips unnoticed into our best actions. … She embellishes our works, adorning them with her own merits and virtues.… She presents these good works to Jesus Christ; for she keeps nothing of what is given to her for herself.… She faithfully passes it all on to Jesus. (*TD*, 146-148)

Suggested Resolutions for Today

- *Set out anew to make the pursuit of God's will your primary concern.*

- *Consider Mary's new resolve in the moments following the angel Gabriel's visit to her. Are there any new directions or changes that God is calling you to make as you seek his will?*

- *Cultivate a habit of offering all your thoughts, works, and desires to Mary so that, offered through her Immaculate Heart, they may be purified, embellished, and presented to Jesus. Allow this to motivate you to proceed with greater confidence toward your consecration.*

Close Your Time of Prayer

With thanksgiving in your heart, pray with Mary the Magnificat and the Glory Be.

DAY 12

Salt
and Light

Begin Your Prayer

Pray the Angelus as an act of presence: Consider the Father's loving gaze upon you, Jesus becoming present to you in Mary, and the Holy Spirit overshadowing you.

Pray for the Light of the Holy Spirit: Pray the *Veni Creator Spiritus*, asking and trusting that the Holy Spirit guide, enrich, and inspire your time of prayer.

Form your desire: To experience a renewed joy and encouragement in continuing to prepare for Marian consecration.

Contemplation

Read slowly and reflectively from Scripture:

"You are the salt of the earth; but if salt has lost its taste, how shall its saltiness be restored? It is no longer good for anything except to be thrown out and trodden under foot by men.

"You are the light of the world. A city set on a hill cannot be hidden. Nor do men light a lamp and put it under a bushel, but on a stand, and it gives light to all in the house. Let your light so shine before men, that they may see your good works and give glory to your Father who is in heaven." (Mt 5:13-16)

From Blessed John Paul II:

The images of salt and light used by Jesus are rich in meaning, and complement each other. In ancient times, salt and light were seen as essential elements of life. "You are the salt of the earth . . . " One of the main functions of salt is to season food, to give it taste and flavor. This image reminds us that, through baptism, our whole being has been profoundly changed, because it has been "seasoned" with the new life which comes from Christ.

The salt which keeps our Christian identity intact, even in a very secularized world, is the grace of baptism. Through baptism, we are reborn. We begin to live in Christ and become capable of responding to His call to "offer [our] bodies as a living sacrifice, holy and acceptable to God" (Rom 12:1). . . .

It is the nature of human beings, and especially youth, to seek the Absolute, the meaning and fullness of life. Dear young people, do not be content with anything less than the highest ideals! Do not let yourselves be dispirited by those who are disillusioned with life, and have grown deaf to the deepest and most authentic desires of their heart. You are right to be disappointed with hollow entertainment and passing fads, and with aiming at too little in life. If you have an ardent desire for the Lord, you will steer clear of the mediocrity and conformism so widespread in our society.

"You are the light of the world ..." For those who first heard Jesus, as for us, the symbol of light evokes the desire for truth and the thirst for the fullness of knowledge which are imprinted deep within every human being.... Our personal encounter with Christ bathes life in new light, sets us on the right path, and sends us out to be his witnesses. (*Message for World Youth Day XVII*, 2001)

- *Return to the words and phrases to which you are most drawn by the Lord. Ponder them reflectively.*

- *Pray from your heart, conversing with the Father, Jesus, the Holy Spirit, and/or Mary.*

- *Pause and receive from God in some time of silent prayer.*

Resolutions for Forming a Life of Marian Consecration

On this final preliminary day of preparation, we consider that our life of consecration is meant to be a light to others and to glorify God. It seeks to bring out and announce the consecration that we have already received in baptism. According to Saint Louis de Montfort, a longing to give greater glory to God can motivate us to consecrate ourselves to Jesus through Mary.

> Our Blessed Lady ... knows most perfectly where the greater glory of God is to be found; and inasmuch as she never does anything except for the greater glory of God, a perfect servant of that good Mistress, who is wholly consecrated to her, may say with the hardiest assurance that the value of all his actions, thoughts and words, is employed for the greater glory of God, unless he purposely revokes his offering. Is there any consolation equal to this for a soul who loves God with a pure and disinterested love, and who prizes the glory and interest of God far beyond his own? (*TD*, 151)

Suggested Resolutions for Today

- *Review the past twelve preliminary days. Consider the most significant graces that you have received or the areas that may still challenge you. Converse lovingly with Mary about these areas. Summarize these in your journal.*

- *Rededicate yourself with renewed generosity as you continue into the first week of preparation.*

Close Your Time of Prayer

With thanksgiving in your heart, pray with Mary the Magnificat and the Glory Be.

FIRST WEEK

Knowledge of Self

Following the preliminary days, the first week of the preparation for total consecration is dedicated to acquiring greater self-knowledge. For Saint Louis de Montfort, this meant developing a profound humility whereby we are aware of our utter nothingness before God and our dependence on him. Strongly convinced of our misery and helplessness, we turn, eager to receive everything from Jesus and Mary.

According to Blessed John Paul II, we come to greater self-knowledge through a contemplation of Jesus Christ. This contemplation reveals what we are *not*, but also who we are called to be. Jesus enters into the depths of our human situation to redeem us. He becomes the New Adam and in doing so his entire life — all that he said and did, especially his passion, death and resurrection — shows the Father to us. By his life and in his actions, Jesus fully reveals man to himself. We learn from him what it means to be created in the image and likeness of God, and we discover in Jesus the true paths of love, communion, and freedom.

Take a moment to re-familiarize yourself with the movements of prayer for each day. Now is a good time to fine-tune your practice of prayer.

- Pray the Angelus as an act of presence, perhaps imaginatively placing yourself in the room of the Annunciation at Nazareth. Become reverently attentive to Mary's presence and the presence of each member of the Trinity.

- The first week employs the Litany of the Holy Spirit as a prayer for light. Have a sense of the Holy Spirit shining more brightly in your heart and mind with each invocation, building your confidence and trust.

- Form your desire by starting with the one suggested, repeating it to yourself, and then customizing it until it's your own. Forming your desire will help you to receive more in prayer.

- In the contemplation, be attentive to the various steps of reading the texts, noticing the words and phrases that jump out to you, pondering them reflectively, speaking to God (any or all of the members of the Trinity) and Mary as your heart is moved, and, last, staying in silence to receive God's love. Resist any restlessness that urges you to move on too quickly.

- The resolutions are there to help you bridge your prayer into your life and thus form, even if gradually, a meaningful and fruitful life of consecration.

- The concluding prayer for the first week is the Memorare. This is a confident prayer beseeching Mary's intercession. Pray it for the intentions of greater self-knowledge and diligence in your resolutions.

PRAYERS TO BE USED
DURING THE FIRST WEEK

Angelus

V. The angel of the Lord declared unto Mary.

R. And she conceived by the power of the Holy Spirit.

  Hail Mary ...

V. Behold the handmaid of the Lord.

R. Be it done unto me according to your Word.

Hail Mary ...

V. And the Word was made flesh.

R. And dwelt among us.

Hail Mary ...

V. Pray for us, O Holy Mother of God.

R. That we may be made worthy of the promises of Christ.

Let us pray. Pour forth, we beseech you, O Lord, your grace into our hearts, that we to whom the incarnation of Christ your Son was made known by the message of an angel, may by his Passion and Cross be brought to the glory of his resurrection; through the same Christ our Lord. Amen.

Litany of the Holy Spirit

Lord, *have mercy on us.*

Christ, *have mercy on us.*

Lord, *have mercy on us.*

Father all powerful, *have mercy on us.*

Jesus, Eternal Son of the Father, Redeemer of the world, *save us.*

Spirit of the Father and the Son, boundless life of both, *sanctify us.*

Holy Trinity, *hear us.*

Holy Spirit, who proceeds from the Father and the Son, *enter our hearts.*

Holy Spirit, equal to the Father and the Son, *enter our hearts.*

Promise of God the Father, *have mercy on us.*

Ray of heavenly light ...

Author of all good ...

Source of heavenly water, *have mercy on us.*
Consuming fire ...
Ardent charity ...
Spiritual unction ...
Spirit of love and truth ...
Spirit of wisdom and understanding ...
Spirit of counsel and fortitude ...
Spirit of knowledge and piety ...
Spirit of the fear of the Lord ...
Spirit of grace and prayer ...
Spirit of peace and meekness ...
Spirit of modesty and innocence ...
Holy Spirit, the Comforter ...
Holy Spirit, the Sanctifier ...
Holy Spirit, who governs the Church ...
Gift of God, the Most High ...
Spirit who fills the universe ...
Spirit of the adoption of the children of God ...

Holy Spirit, *inspire us with horror of sin.*
Holy Spirit, *come and renew the face of the earth.*
Holy Spirit, *shed your light in our souls.*
Holy Spirit, *engrave your law in our hearts.*
Holy Spirit, *inflame us with the flame of your love.*
Holy Spirit, *open to us the treasures of your graces.*
Holy Spirit, *teach us to pray well.*
Holy Spirit, *enlighten us with your heavenly inspirations.*
Holy Spirit, *lead us in the way of salvation.*
Holy Spirit, *grant us the only necessary knowledge.*
Holy Spirit, *inspire in us the practice of good.*
Holy Spirit, *grant us the merits of all virtues.*
Holy Spirit, *make us persevere in justice.*
Holy Spirit, *be our everlasting reward.*

Lamb of God, who takes away the sins of the world,
    Send us your Holy Spirit.

Lamb of God, who takes away the sins of the world,

Pour down into our souls the gifts of the Holy Spirit.

Lamb of God, who takes away the sins of the world,
Grant us the Spirit of wisdom and piety.

V. Come, Holy Spirit! Fill the hearts of your faithful,
R. *And enkindle in them the fire of your love.*

Let us pray. Grant, O merciful Father, that your Divine
Spirit may enlighten, inflame and purify us, that He may
penetrate us with His heavenly dew and make us fruitful
in good works, through Our Lord Jesus Christ, your Son,
who with you, in the unity of the same Spirit, lives and
reigns forever and ever. Amen.

Memorare of the Blessed Virgin Mary

Remember, O most gracious Virgin Mary,
that never was it known
that anyone who fled to your protection,
implored your help, or sought your intercession
was left unaided.
Inspired by this confidence,
I fly unto you, O Virgin of virgins, my mother.
To you do I come, before you I stand,
sinful and sorrowful.
O Mother of the Word Incarnate,
despise not my petitions,
but in your mercy, hear and answer me.
Amen.

DAY 13

Christ Fully
Reveals You to Yourself

Begin Your Prayer

Pray the Angelus as an act of presence: Consider the Father's loving gaze upon you, Jesus becoming present to you in Mary, and the Holy Spirit overshadowing you.

Pray for the Light of the Holy Spirit: Pray the Litany of the Holy Spirit with a sense of the Holy Spirit gently penetrating ever deeper into your heart with each invocation.

Form your desire: To know yourself as Jesus knows you.

Contemplation

Read slowly and reflectively from Scripture:

> At that time Jesus declared, "I thank you, Father, Lord of heaven and earth, that you have hidden these things from the wise and understanding and revealed them to infants; yes, Father, for such was your gracious will. All things have been delivered to me by my Father; and no one knows the Son except the Father, and no one knows the Father except the Son and any one to whom the Son chooses to reveal him. Come to me, all who labor and are heavy laden, and I will give you rest. Take my yoke upon you, and learn from me; for I am gentle and lowly in heart, and you will find rest for your souls. For my yoke is easy, and my burden is light. (Mt 11:25-30)
>
> Blessed be the God and Father of our Lord Jesus Christ, who has blessed us in Christ with every spiritual blessing in the heavenly places, even as he chose us in him before

the foundation of the world, that we should be holy and blameless before him.

He destined us in love to be his sons through Jesus Christ, according to the purpose of his will, to the praise of his glorious grace which he freely bestowed on us in the Beloved. In him we have redemption through his blood, the forgiveness of our trespasses, according to the riches of his grace which he lavished upon us. (Eph 1:3-8)

From Blessed John Paul II:

Christ, the Redeemer of the world, is the one who penetrated in a unique unrepeatable way into the mystery of man and entered his "heart." Rightly therefore does the Second Vatican Council teach: "The truth is that only in the mystery of the Incarnate Word does the mystery of man take on light. For Adam, the first man, was a type of him who was to come (Rom 5:14), Christ the Lord. Christ the new Adam, in the very revelation of the mystery of the Father and of his love, fully reveals man to himself and brings to light his most high calling."

And the council continues: "He who is the 'image of the invisible God' (Col 1:15), is himself the perfect man who has restored in the children of Adam that likeness to God which had been disfigured ever since the first sin. Human nature, by the very fact that it was assumed, not absorbed, in him, has been raised in us also to a dignity beyond compare. For, by his Incarnation, he, the son of God, in a certain way united himself with each man. He worked with human hands, he thought with a human mind. He acted with a human will, and with a human heart he loved. Born of the Virgin Mary, he has truly been made one of us, like to us in all things except sin" (*GS*, 22), he, the Redeemer of man. (*RH*, 8)

- *Return to the words and phrases to which you are most drawn by the Lord. Ponder them reflectively.*

- *Pray from your heart, conversing with the Father, Jesus, the Holy Spirit, and/or Mary.*

- *Pause and receive from God in some time of silent prayer.*

Resolutions for Forming a Life of Marian Consecration

The first week of preparation is focused on gaining knowledge of self. One of Blessed John Paul II's most frequently quoted passages from the Second Vatican Council is from the Constitution on the Church in the Modern World (*Gaudium et Spes*): Jesus Christ "fully reveals man to himself" (22). As we pray during this week for self-knowledge let us begin by recalling his familiar words — "Be not afraid!" — and turn to Christ who will reveal us to ourselves.

> "Have no fear!" Do not be afraid of God's mystery; do not be afraid of His love; and do not be afraid of man's weakness or of his grandeur! Man does not cease to be great, not even in his weakness. Do not be afraid of being witnesses to the dignity of every human being, from the moment of conception until death. (*CTH*, p. 12)

Suggested Resolutions for Today

- *Continue to form a habitual sense of Mary's presence beside you. Frequently turn to her throughout the day.*

- *Resolve to form a life of Marian consecration that is based on finding your identity in Christ. Hear Christ's words echoed by John Paul II, "Be not afraid!" spoken to your soul.*

Close Your Time of Prayer

With gratitude in your heart, pray the Memorare, asking for Mary's intercession that you may grow in self-knowledge and remain diligent in your resolutions.

DAY 14

The Baptism of Jesus and Our Baptismal Identity

Begin Your Prayer

Pray the Angelus as an act of presence: Consider the Father's loving gaze upon you, Jesus becoming present to you in Mary, and the Holy Spirit overshadowing you.

Pray for the Light of the Holy Spirit: Pray the Litany of the Holy Spirit with a sense of the Holy Spirit gently penetrating ever deeper into your heart with each invocation.

Form your desire: To come to a greater knowledge of how, by baptism, you are a beloved son or daughter of God.

Contemplation

Read slowly and reflectively from Scripture:

> Then Jesus came from Galilee to the Jordan to John, to be baptized by him. John would have prevented him, saying, "I need to be baptized by you, and do you come to me?" But Jesus answered him, "Let it be so now; for thus it is fitting for us to fulfil all righteousness." Then he consented. And when Jesus was baptized, he went up immediately from the water, and behold, the heavens were opened and he saw the Spirit of God descending like a dove, and alighting on him; and behold, a voice from heaven, saying, "This is my beloved Son, with whom I am well pleased." (Mt 3:13-17)

See what love the Father has given us, that we should be called children of God; and so we are. The reason why the world does not know us is that it did not know him.

Beloved, we are God's children now; it does not yet appear what we shall be, but we know that when he appears we shall be like him, for we shall see him as he is. (1 Jn 3:1-2)

From Blessed John Paul II:

It is no exaggeration to say that the entire existence of the lay faithful has as its purpose to lead a person to a knowledge of the radical newness of the Christian life that comes from baptism, the sacrament of faith, so that this knowledge can help that person live the responsibilities which arise from that vocation received from God.... Baptism regenerates us in the life of the Son of God; unites us to Christ and to his Body, the Church; anoints us in the Holy Spirit, making us spiritual temples....

With baptism we become *children of God in his only-begotten Son, Jesus Christ.* Rising from the waters of the baptismal font, every Christian hears again the voice that was once heard on the banks of the Jordan River: "You are my beloved Son; with you I am well pleased" (Lk 3:22). From this comes the understanding that one has been brought into association with the beloved Son, becoming a child of adoption (cf. Gal 4:4-7) and a brother or sister of Christ. (*CL*, 10-11)

- *Return to the words and phrases to which you are most drawn by the Lord. Ponder them reflectively.*

- *Pray from your heart, conversing with the Father, Jesus, the Holy Spirit, and/or Mary.*

- *Pause and receive from God in some time of silent prayer.*

Resolutions for Forming a Life of Marian Consecration

For Saint Louis de Montfort, total consecration is synonymous with "a perfect renewal of the vows and promises of holy baptism" (*TD*, 120). Baptism is our fundamental consecration. Through the waters of baptism, we are born into the new life of

Christ. We become adopted sons and daughters of God the Father and temples of the Holy Spirit. Whether our baptism took place as an infant or as an adult, total consecration activates our faith in the present and renews our commitment to Christ at its core. It enables us to choose more fully and consciously our baptismal call to holiness.

Suggested Resolutions for Today

- *Take a moment either now or later today to renew your baptismal promises by praying the Apostles' Creed or the Profession of Faith from Mass. Consider how your promises may become more than mere statements of belief, but lived-out statements of faith.*

- *Resolve to form a life of Marian consecration that lives out of the reality that you are a beloved son or daughter of God.*

Close Your Time of Prayer

With gratitude in your heart, pray the Memorare, asking for Mary's intercession that you may grow in self-knowledge and remain diligent in your resolutions.

DAY 15

Call to Holiness

Begin Your Prayer

Pray the Angelus as an act of presence: Consider the Father's loving gaze upon you, Jesus becoming present to you in Mary, and the Holy Spirit overshadowing you.

Pray for the Light of the Holy Spirit: Pray the Litany of the Holy Spirit with a sense of the Holy Spirit gently penetrating ever deeper into your heart with each invocation.

Form your desire: To feel a greater yearning in your heart to respond to Jesus calling you to holiness.

Contemplation

Read slowly and reflectively from Scripture:

"You, therefore, must be perfect, as your heavenly Father is perfect." (Mt 5:48)

And as he was setting out on his journey, a man ran up and knelt before him, and asked him, "Good Teacher, what must I do to inherit eternal life?" And Jesus said to him, "Why do you call me good? No one is good but God alone. You know the commandments: 'Do not kill, Do not commit adultery, Do not steal, Do not bear false witness, Do not defraud, Honor your father and mother.'" And he said to him, "Teacher, all these I have observed from my youth." And Jesus looking upon him loved him, and said to him, "You lack one thing; go, sell what you have, and give to the poor, and you will have treasure in heaven; and come, follow me." At that saying his countenance fell, and he went away sorrowful; for he had great possessions. (Mk 10:17-22)

From Blessed John Paul II:

We come to a full sense of the dignity of the lay faithful if we consider *the prime and fundamental vocation* that the Father assigns to each of them in Jesus Christ through the Holy Spirit: the vocation to holiness, that is, the perfection of charity. Holiness is the greatest testimony of the dignity conferred on a disciple of Christ. (*LC*, 16)

Following Christ ... is not a matter only of disposing oneself to hear a teaching and obediently accepting a commandment. More radically, it involves *holding fast to the very person of Jesus*, partaking of his life and destiny, sharing in his free and loving obedience to the will of the Father. ... *Following Christ* is not an outward imitation, since it touches man at the very depths of his being. Being a follower of Christ means *becoming conformed to him* who became a servant even to giving himself on the cross.

Christ dwells by faith in the heart of the believer, and thus the disciple is conformed to the Lord. This is the *effect of grace*, of the active presence of the Holy Spirit in us. (*VS*, 19, 21)

- *Return to the words and phrases to which you are most drawn by the Lord. Ponder them reflectively.*

- *Pray from your heart, conversing with the Father, Jesus, the Holy Spirit, and/or Mary.*

- *Pause and receive from God in some time of silent prayer.*

Resolutions for Forming a Life of Marian Consecration

Each of us is called to holiness. Forming a life of Marian consecration is a particular way of responding to that call, no matter what our state in life. Holiness is actually a gift from God.

It means not restricting the action of grace within us, but responding like Mary. We can learn from Mary the pathways of holiness as Saint Louis de Montfort says:

> True devotion to Our Lady is holy, that is to say, it leads the soul to avoid sin and to imitate the virtues of the Blessed Virgin, particularly her profound humility, her lively faith, her blind obedience, her continual prayer, her universal mortification, her divine purity, her ardent charity, her heroic patience, her angelic sweetness, and her divine wisdom. These are the ten principal virtues of the most holy Virgin. (*TD*, 108)

Suggested Resolutions for Today

- *Throughout today, endeavor to see your simple and ordinary tasks and encounters as opportunities to respond to grace and live out holiness.*

- *Resolve to live a holy life in Marian consecration. This entails letting your love of Jesus and Mary strengthen you in the struggle against sin, getting up confidently when you fall, and imitating the virtues and self-giving love of Mary.*

Close Your Time of Prayer

With gratitude in your heart, pray the Memorare, asking for Mary's intercession that you may grow in self-knowledge and remain diligent in your resolutions.

DAY 16

Gift of Self

Begin Your Prayer

Pray the Angelus as an act of presence: Consider the Father's loving gaze upon you, Jesus becoming present to you in Mary, and the Holy Spirit overshadowing you.

Pray for the Light of the Holy Spirit: Pray the Litany of the Holy Spirit with a sense of the Holy Spirit gently penetrating ever deeper into your heart with each invocation.

Form your desire: To experience awe and wonder at being created in God's image and likeness and being called to love through a "gift of self."

Contemplation

Read slowly and reflectively from Scripture:

God created man in his own image, in the image of God he created him; male and female he created them. (Gn 1:27)

Then the Lord God said, "It is not good that the man should be alone; I will make him a helper fit for him." So out of the ground the Lord God formed every beast of the field and every bird of the air, and brought them to the man to see what he would call them; and whatever the man called every living creature, that was its name. The man gave names to all cattle, and to the birds of the air, and to every beast of the field; but for the man there was not found a helper fit for him.

So the Lord God caused a deep sleep to fall upon the man, and while he slept took one of his ribs and closed up its place with flesh; and the rib which the Lord God had taken from the man he made into a woman and brought her to the man. Then the man said,

> "This at last is bone of my bones
> and flesh of my flesh;
> she shall be called Woman,
> because she was taken out of Man."

Therefore a man leaves his father and his mother and cleaves to his wife, and they become one flesh. And the man and his wife were both naked, and were not ashamed. (Gn 2:18-25)

From Blessed John Paul II:

Man becomes an image of God not so much in the moment of solitude as in the moment of communion. He is, in fact, "from the beginning" not only an image of God in which the solitude of one Person, who rules the world, mirrors itself, but also and essentially the image of an inscrutable divine communion of Persons (*Gen. Aud. [Theology of the Body]*, November 14, 1979).

The human body, with its sex — its masculinity and femininity — seen in the very mystery of creation, is not only a source of fruitfulness and of procreation, as in the whole natural order, but contains "from the beginning" the "spousal" attribute, that is, *the power to express love: precisely that love in which the human person becomes gift* and — through this gift — fulfills the very meaning of his being and existence.

We recall here the text of the most recent council in which it declares that man is the only creature in the visible world that God willed "for its own sake," adding that this man cannot "fully find himself except through a sincere gift of self" (*GS*, 24). (*Gen. Aud. [Theology of the Body]*, January 16, 1980).

- *Return to the words and phrases to which you are most drawn by the Lord. Ponder them reflectively.*

- *Pray from your heart, conversing with the Father, Jesus, the Holy Spirit, and/or Mary.*

- *Pause and receive from God in some time of silent prayer.*

Resolutions for Forming a Life of Marian Consecration

Saint Louis de Montfort describes true devotion to Mary as a holy slavery by which we give everything we are entirely to Mary. Blessed John Paul II speaks of the total gift of self. Entrustment to Mary is making a total gift of self to Mary and believing that she gives all that she is to us. Saint Louis de Montfort says:

> The most holy Virgin, who is Mother of sweetness and mercy, and who never lets herself be outdone in love and liberality ... gives her whole self, and gives it in an unspeakable manner, to him who gives all to her. (*TD*, 144).

Suggested Resolutions for Today

- *Often our tendency is to selfishly orient our lives back toward ourselves; we tend to take, grasp, or make use of persons and things for our own needs, desires, preferences, and pleasures. In your thoughts and interactions with others today, seek to orient and direct yourself toward giving the gift of self especially through opportunities for sacrificial love.*

- *Consider throughout this day Mary's desire to give herself to you. Resolve to form a life of Marian consecration that is a reciprocal gift of self. This entails entrusting all that you are to Mary with a generous love.*

Close Your Time of Prayer

With gratitude in your heart, pray the Memorare, asking for Mary's intercession that you may grow in self-knowledge and remain diligent in your resolutions.

DAY 17

Communion

Begin Your Prayer

Pray the Angelus as an act of presence: Consider the Father's loving gaze upon you, Jesus becoming present to you in Mary, and the Holy Spirit overshadowing you.

Pray for the Light of the Holy Spirit: Pray the Litany of the Holy Spirit with a sense of the Holy Spirit gently penetrating ever deeper into your heart with each invocation.

Form your desire: To experience loving union with Jesus and Mary.

Contemplation

Read slowly and reflectively from Scripture:

"I am the true vine, and my Father is the vinedresser. Every branch of mine that bears no fruit, he takes away, and every branch that does bear fruit he prunes, that it may bear more fruit. You are already made clean by the word which I have spoken to you. Abide in me, and I in you. As the branch cannot bear fruit by itself, unless it abides in the vine, neither can you, unless you abide in me. I am the vine, you are the branches. He who abides in me, and I in him, he it is that bears much fruit, for apart from me you can do nothing. If a man does not abide in me, he is cast forth as a branch and withers; and the branches are gathered, thrown into the fire and burned. If you abide in me, and my words abide in you, ask whatever you will, and it shall be done for you. By this my Father is glorified, that you bear much fruit, and so prove to be my disciples." (Jn 15:1-8)

From Blessed John Paul II:

Again we turn to the words of Jesus: "I am the true vine and my Father is the vinedresser.... Abide in me and I in you" (Jn 15:1,4). These simple words reveal the mystery of communion that serves as the unifying bond between the Lord and his disciples, between Christ and the baptized — a living and life-giving communion through which Christians no longer belong to themselves but are the Lord's very own, as the branches are one with the vine.

The communion of Christians with Jesus has the communion of God as Trinity — namely, the unity of the Son to the Father in the gift of the Holy Spirit, as its model and source, and is itself the means to achieve this communion: united to the Son in the Spirit's bond of love, Christians are united to the Father.

Jesus continues: "I am the vine, you are the branches" (Jn 15:5). From the communion that Christians experience in Christ there immediately flows the communion which they experience with one another: all are branches of a single vine, namely, Christ. In this communion is the wonderful reflection and participation in the mystery of the intimate life of love in God as Trinity, Father, Son, and Holy Spirit as revealed by the Lord Jesus.

For this communion Jesus prays: "that they may all be one; even as you, Father, are in me, and I in you, that they also may be in us, so that the world may believe that you have sent me" (Jn 17:21). (CL, 18)

A spirituality of communion also means an ability to think of our brothers and sisters in faith within the profound unity of the Mystical Body, and therefore as "those who are a part of me." This makes us able to share their joys and sufferings, to sense their desires and attend to their needs, to offer them deep and genuine friendship.

A spirituality of communion implies also the ability to see what is positive in others, to welcome it and prize it as a gift from God: not only as a gift for the brother or sister who has received it directly, but also as a "gift for me." A spirituality of communion means, finally, to know how to "make room" for our brothers and sisters, bearing "each other's burdens" (Gal 6:2) and resisting the selfish temptations which constantly beset us and provoke competition, careerism, distrust and jealousy. (*NMI*, 43)

- *Return to the words and phrases to which you are most drawn by the Lord. Ponder them reflectively.*

- *Pray from your heart, conversing with the Father, Jesus, the Holy Spirit, and/or Mary.*

- *Pause and receive from God in some time of silent prayer.*

Resolutions for Forming a Life of Marian Consecration

By our baptism, we are drawn into a life of communion with the Blessed Trinity. We are called to live out communion with one another by being a *gift* for others. A life of Marian consecration is one of communion with Mary that in turn opens our hearts for a greater capacity for communion with God and others.

Saint Louis de Montfort explains that an effect of true devotion is that Mary draws near to us in a unity of love: "The soul of our Blessed Lady will communicate itself to you to glorify the Lord. Her spirit will enter into the place of yours, to rejoice in God her salvation" (*TD*, 217).

Suggested Resolutions for Today

- *In your interactions with others today, see each person as a "gift" for you. Also, strive to "make room" for those who may ordinarily be hard to bear, or may themselves be burdened.*

- *Resolve to form a life of Marian consecration by frequently choosing and entering a loving communion with Mary.*

Close Your Time of Prayer

With gratitude in your heart, pray the Memorare, asking for Mary's intercession that you may grow in self-knowledge and remain diligent in your resolutions.

DAY 18

Love

Begin Your Prayer

Pray the Angelus as an act of presence: Consider the Father's loving gaze upon you, Jesus becoming present to you in Mary, and the Holy Spirit overshadowing you.

Pray for the Light of the Holy Spirit: Pray the Litany of the Holy Spirit with a sense of the Holy Spirit gently penetrating ever deeper into your heart with each invocation.

Form your desire: To experience the joy of friendship with Christ.

Contemplation

Read slowly and reflectively from Scripture:

"As the Father has loved me, so have I loved you; abide in my love. If you keep my commandments, you will abide in my love, just as I have kept my Father's commandments and abide in his love. These things I have spoken to you, that my joy may be in you, and that your joy may be full.

"This is my commandment, that you love one another as I have loved you. Greater love has no man than this, that a man lay down his life for his friends. You are my friends if you do what I command you. No longer do I call you servants, for the servant does not know what his master is doing; but I have called you friends, for all that I have heard from my Father I have made known to you. You did not choose me, but I chose you and appointed you that you should go and bear fruit and that your fruit should abide; so that whatever you ask the Father in my name, he may give it to you. This I command you, to love one another." (Jn 15:9-17)

From Blessed John Paul II:

Man cannot live without love. He remains a being that is incomprehensible for himself, his life is senseless, if love is not revealed to him, if he does not encounter love, if he does not experience it and make it his own, if he does not participate intimately in it. This, as has already been said, is why Christ the Redeemer "fully reveals man to himself"....

The man who wishes to understand himself thoroughly — and not just in accordance with immediate, partial, often superficial, and even illusory standards and measures of his being — he must with his unrest, uncertainty and even his weakness and sinfulness, with his life and death, draw near to Christ. He must, so to speak, enter into him with all his own self, he must "appropriate" and assimilate the whole of the reality of the Incarnation and Redemption in order to find himself.

If this profound process takes place within him, he then bears fruit not only of adoration of God but also of deep wonder at himself. How precious must man be in the eyes of the Creator, if he "gained so great a Redeemer" [*Exsultet* at Easter Vigil], and if God "gave his only Son "in order that man "should not perish but have eternal life" [cf. Jn 3:16]. (*RH*, 10)

- *Return to the words and phrases to which you are most drawn by the Lord. Ponder them reflectively.*

- *Pray from your heart, conversing with the Father, Jesus, the Holy Spirit, and/or Mary.*

- *Pause and receive from God in some time of silent prayer.*

Resolutions for Forming a Life of Marian Consecration

This is the real meaning of life: to love. The world will speak of love in many different ways, but Jesus teaches us specifically to love one another as he loved us. This is challenging. We are to love not just when it is easy, but also when it is difficult — to love sacrificially through a sincere gift of self. But this is not just some task we attempt by imitation, but through communion and friendship with Jesus. We are conformed to Christ through this friendship and enabled to love with *his* love. "We love because he first loved us" (1 Jn 4:19). A life of Marian consecration keeps us centered on Christ that we may be conformed to him. In speaking about the Rosary, Blessed John Paul II said:

> Based on the constant contemplation — in Mary's company — of the face of Christ, this demanding ideal of being conformed to him is pursued through an association which could be described in terms of friendship. We are thereby enabled to enter naturally into Christ's life and as it were to share his deepest feelings. (*RVM*, 15)

Suggested Resolutions for Today

- *Consider how Jesus has loved you. Examine your own life for how you have loved others. Look at your relationships with family, friends, acquaintances, and even strangers.*

- *Continue to foster an interior disposition of remaining with Mary in communion love. Allow this to draw you ever deeper into your friendship with Christ.*

- *Resolve to form a life of Marian consecration that demonstrates its authenticity through loving as Christ loved.*

Close Your Time of Prayer

With gratitude in your heart, pray the Memorare, asking for Mary's intercession that you may grow in self-knowledge and remain diligent in your resolutions.

DAY 19

Freedom

Begin Your Prayer

Pray the Angelus as an act of presence: Consider the Father's loving gaze upon you, Jesus becoming present to you in Mary, and the Holy Spirit overshadowing you.

Pray for the Light of the Holy Spirit: Pray the Litany of the Holy Spirit with a sense of the Holy Spirit gently penetrating ever deeper into your heart with each invocation.

Form your desire: To experience genuine freedom based on the certain truth of God's love for you.

Contemplation

Read slowly and reflectively from Scripture:

> Jesus then said to the Jews who had believed in him, "If you continue in my word, you are truly my disciples, and you will know the truth, and the truth will make you free." (Jn 8:31-32)

> For freedom Christ has set us free; stand fast therefore, and do not submit again to a yoke of slavery. . . . For you were called to freedom, brethren; only do not use your freedom as an opportunity for the flesh, but through love be servants of one another. (Gal 5:1,13)

From Blessed John Paul II:

> Human freedom belongs to us as creatures; it is a freedom which is given as a gift, one to be received like a seed and

to be cultivated responsibly. It is an essential part of that creaturely image which is the basis of the dignity of the person.

Within that freedom there is an echo of the primordial vocation whereby the Creator calls man to the true Good, and even more, through Christ's revelation, to become his friend and to share his own divine life. It is at once inalienable self-possession and openness to all that exists, in passing beyond self to knowledge and love of the other (*GS*, 24).

Freedom then is rooted in the truth about man, and it is ultimately directed toward communion. Reason and experience not only confirm the weakness of human freedom; they also confirm its tragic aspects. Man comes to realize that his freedom is in some mysterious way inclined to betray this openness to the True and the Good, and that all too often he actually prefers to choose finite, limited and ephemeral goods.

What is more, within his errors and negative decisions, man glimpses the source of a deep rebellion, which leads him to reject the Truth and the Good in order to set himself up as an absolute principle unto himself: "You will be like God" (Gn 3:5).

Consequently, freedom itself needs to be set free. It is Christ who sets it free: he "has set us free for freedom" (cf. Gal 5:1). (*VS*, 86)

- *Return to the words and phrases to which you are most drawn by the Lord. Ponder them reflectively.*

- *Pray from your heart, conversing with the Father, Jesus, the Holy Spirit, and/or Mary.*

- *Pause and receive from God in some time of silent prayer.*

Resolutions for Forming a Life of Marian Consecration

In developing a life of Marian consecration whereby we give the total gift of self to Mary — or in the words of Saint Louis de Montfort, give oursleves in holy slavery — it would seem that we would be diminishing our freedom. But the contrary is actually true. Genuine freedom is not the right or ability to do whatever I want, but the ability to do the good that I *should* do. Loving obedience to the will of God always frees us for the good. Mary demonstrates this true freedom in her free consent to God's will at the Annunciation: "Let it be to me according to your word" (Lk 1:38). Marian consecration, therefore, frees us for greater love. Blessed John Paul II noted the dynamic of love and its relationship to freedom in Jesus' life:

> Jesus reveals by his whole life, and not only by his words, that freedom is acquired in love, that is, in the gift of self. The one who says: "Greater love has no man than this, that a man lay down his life for his friends" (Jn 15:13), freely goes out to meet his Passion, and in obedience to the Father gives his life on the Cross for all men. (*VS*, 87)

Suggested Resolutions for Today

- *Review the past week. Consider the most significant graces you have received, or perhaps areas that may still challenge you. Converse lovingly with Mary about these. Summarize them in your journal.*

- *Consider where in your life you may not be free. Reveal these areas to Mary.*

- *Resolve to form a life of Marian consecration that is free. This entails a genuine freedom based on truth and not merely preserving one's own preferences.*

Close Your Time of Prayer

With gratitude in your heart, pray the Memorare, asking for Mary's intercession that you may grow in self-knowledge and remain diligent in your resolutions.

SECOND WEEK

Knowledge of Mary

The second week of preparation for total consecration is dedicated to gaining a loving knowledge of Mary. The Scripture passages for this week's contemplations center on episodes from her life. Though these stories may be familiar, we trust the Holy Spirit to guide our prayer so that we may discover and know Mary in a new and deeper way. We will attune ourselves to Mary's interior life — her virtues, her prayer, her sentiments, her actions, and her loving union with Jesus. By drawing nearer to Mary, we enter into her contemplation of Christ. Thus we'll discover that as we grow in loving knowledge of Mary, she will naturally lead us to a greater love and knowledge of her Son.

Once again, as you begin a new week, take a look at the steps of prayer for each day. Review the different movements — the act of presence, prayer for light, and so forth. These will mostly stay the same for this week, but it is good to examine how you have been praying them and recommit yourself to praying them well. Changes for the second week include the addition of a daily Rosary, and a different concluding prayer which is addressed to Mary and has been adapted from one written by Saint Louis de Montfort. It is essentially a prayer of communion that highlights Mary's relationship with the Trinity and expresses the desire to grow in a deeper loving communion with her.

A goal of the second week is to begin to pray the Rosary every day. This is a practice that we hope to continue into our new life of Marian consecration. In our resolutions, we will be attentive to forming the disciplined habit of praying a daily Rosary in such a way that it is not a burdensome or mechanical task, but rather an enriching and fruitful part of our interior life that sustains our consecration to Jesus through Mary. In his apostolic letter on the Rosary, *Rosarium Virginis Mariae*, Blessed John Paul II teaches us to pray the Rosary contemplatively: "The Rosary, precisely because it starts with Mary's own experiences, is an *exquisitely contemplative prayer*. Without this contemplative dimension, it would lose its meaning" (*RVM*, 12).

As you pray the Rosary this week, be particularly attentive to the mystery being contemplated. Allow yourself to be drawn into Mary's contemplation of Christ. You may choose to imaginatively place yourself in the scene or simply ponder Mary's sentiments and actions. All the while, allow the Our Fathers, Hail Marys, and Glory Bes to set a gentle rhythm that draws you back from any distraction. Be attentive to taking times of silence to dispose your heart, take in a loving gaze, pause in awe, or receive God's love. Pray the Rosary as a genuine act of love — an expression of your total gift of self to Mary.

PRAYERS TO BE USED DURING
THE SECOND WEEK

Angelus

V. The angel of the Lord declared unto Mary.

R. And she conceived by the power of the Holy Spirit.
Hail Mary ...

V. Behold the handmaid of the Lord.

R. Be it done unto me according to your Word.
Hail Mary ...

V. And the Word was made flesh.

R. And dwelt among us.

Hail Mary ...

V. Pray for us, O Holy Mother of God.

R. That we may be made worthy of the promises of Christ.

Let us pray.

Pour forth, we beseech you, O Lord, your grace into our hearts, that we to whom the incarnation of Christ your Son was made known by the message of an angel, may by his Passion and Cross be brought to the glory of his resurrection; through the same Christ our Lord. Amen.

Litany of the Holy Spirit

Lord, *have mercy on us.*
Christ, *have mercy on us.*
Lord, *have mercy on us.*
Father all powerful, *have mercy on us.*
Jesus, Eternal Son of the Father, Redeemer of the world, *save us.*
Spirit of the Father and the Son, boundless life of both, *sanctify us.*
Holy Trinity, *hear us.*

Holy Spirit, who proceeds from the Father and the Son, *enter our hearts.*
Holy Spirit, equal to the Father and the Son, *enter our hearts.*

Promise of God the Father, *have mercy on us.*
Ray of heavenly light ...
Author of all good ...
Source of heavenly water ...
Consuming fire ...
Ardent charity ...

Spiritual unction, *have mercy on us*
Spirit of love and truth ...
Spirit of wisdom and understanding ...
Spirit of counsel and fortitude ...
Spirit of knowledge and piety ...
Spirit of the fear of the Lord ...
Spirit of grace and prayer ...
Spirit of peace and meekness ...
Spirit of modesty and innocence ...
Holy Spirit, the Comforter ...
Holy Spirit, the Sanctifier ...
Holy Spirit, who governs the Church ...
Gift of God, the Most High ...
Spirit who fills the universe ...
Spirit of the adoption of the children of God ...

Holy Spirit, *inspire us with horror of sin.*
Holy Spirit, *come and renew the face of the earth.*
Holy Spirit, *shed your light in our souls.*
Holy Spirit, *engrave your law in our hearts.*
Holy Spirit, *inflame us with the flame of your love.*
Holy Spirit, *open to us the treasures of your graces.*
Holy Spirit, *teach us to pray well.*
Holy Spirit, *enlighten us with your heavenly inspirations.*
Holy Spirit, *lead us in the way of salvation.*
Holy Spirit, *grant us the only necessary knowledge.*
Holy Spirit, *inspire in us the practice of good.*
Holy Spirit, *grant us the merits of all virtues.*
Holy Spirit, *make us persevere in justice.*
Holy Spirit, *be our everlasting reward.*

Lamb of God, who takes away the sins of the world,
    Send us your Holy Spirit.

Lamb of God, who takes away the sins of the world,
    Pour down into our souls the gifts of the Holy Spirit.

Lamb of God, who takes away the sins of the world,
    Grant us the Spirit of wisdom and piety.

V. Come, Holy Spirit! Fill the hearts of your faithful,
R. *And enkindle in them the fire of your love.*

Let us pray. Grant, O merciful Father, that your Divine Spirit may enlighten, inflame and purify us, that He may penetrate us with His heavenly dew and make us fruitful in good works, through Our Lord Jesus Christ, your Son, who with you, in the unity of the same Spirit, lives and reigns forever and ever. Amen.

Prayer to Mary for the Second Week

(adapted from Saint Louis de Montfort)

Hail Mary, beloved Daughter of God the Father! Hail Mary, admirable Mother of Jesus the Son! Hail Mary, faithful Spouse of the Holy Spirit! Hail Mary, my Mother, the joy of my heart and soul! I give myself wholly to you.

By your loving presence with me, take from within me all that may displease God. Place and cultivate within me everything that delights Him in you. May the light of your faith dispel the darkness of my mind. May your humility take the place of my pride. May your contemplative beholding of Jesus fill my heart. May the burning love of your heart inflame the lukewarmness of mine. May your virtues take the place of my sins. May I join my "yes" to yours and have no greater desires than to know and love Jesus and to do the Father's will.

I do not ask you for spiritual favors and heights beyond me. I desire only to receive the love you have for me. With such grace then may my heart resound at every moment of the day, and every moment of my life. Amen, so be it, to all that you are doing in heaven. Amen, so be it, to all you did while on earth. Amen, so be it, to all you are doing in my soul, so that you may glorify Jesus in me now and forever. Amen.

DAY 20

The Annunciation

Begin Your Prayer

Pray the Angelus as an act of presence: Consider the Father's loving gaze upon you, Jesus becoming present to you in Mary, and the Holy Spirit overshadowing you.

Pray for the Light of the Holy Spirit: Pray the Litany of the Holy Spirit with a sense of the Holy Spirit gently penetrating ever deeper into your heart with each invocation.

Form your desire: To feel your heart expand and open to Mary.

Contemplation

Read slowly and reflectively from Scripture:

> In the sixth month the angel Gabriel was sent from God to a city of Galilee named Nazareth, to a virgin betrothed to a man whose name was Joseph, of the house of David; and the virgin's name was Mary. And he came to her and said, "Hail, full of grace, the Lord is with you!" But she was greatly troubled at the saying, and considered in her mind what sort of greeting this might be.
>
> And the angel said to her, "Do not be afraid, Mary, for you have found favor with God. And behold, you will conceive in your womb and bear a son, and you shall call his name Jesus. He will be great, and will be called the Son of the Most High; and the Lord God will give to him the throne of his father David, and he will reign over the house of Jacob for ever; and of his kingdom there will be no end."
>
> And Mary said to the angel, "How shall this be, since I have no husband?" And the angel said to her, "The Holy Spirit will come upon you, and the power of the Most High

will overshadow you; therefore the child to be born will be called holy, the Son of God. And behold, your kinswoman Elizabeth in her old age has also conceived a son; and this is the sixth month with her who was called barren. For with God nothing will be impossible." And Mary said, "Behold, I am the handmaid of the Lord; let it be to me according to your word." And the angel departed from her. (Lk 1:26-38)

From Blessed John Paul II:

It is significant that Mary, recognizing in the words of the divine messenger the will of the Most High and submitting to his power, says: "Behold, I am the handmaid of the Lord; let it be to me according to your word" (Lk 1:38). The first moment of submission to the one mediation "between God and men" — the mediation of Jesus Christ — is the Virgin of Nazareth's acceptance of motherhood. Mary consents to God's choice, in order to become through the power of the Holy Spirit the Mother of the Son of God.

It can be said that a consent to motherhood is above all a result of her total self-giving to God in virginity. Mary accepted her election as Mother of the Son of God, guided by spousal love, the love which totally "consecrates" a human being to God. By virtue of this love, Mary wished to be always and in all things "given to God," living in virginity.

The words "Behold, I am the handmaid of the Lord" express the fact that from the outset she accepted and understood her own motherhood as a total gift of self, a gift of her person to the service of the saving plans of the Most High. (*RM*, 39)

- *Return to the words and phrases to which you are most drawn by the Lord. Ponder them reflectively.*

- *Pray from your heart, conversing with the Father, Jesus, the Holy Spirit, and/or Mary.*

- *Pause and receive from God in some time of silent prayer.*

99

Resolutions for Forming a Life of Marian Consecration

In the mystery of the Annunciation, we see in Mary a total self-giving love that results in her free consent to God's plan. John Paul II says such love has a spousal character that "totally consecrates a human being to God." This week is devoted to gaining a deep and personal knowledge of Mary. Knowing Our Lady, especially in her total gift of self, will draw us into *her* consecration. Thus we desire to enter into the heart of Mary and her interior life. This will lead us to a greater love and contemplation of Christ as John Paul II explains:

> The contemplation of Christ has an *incomparable model* in Mary. In a unique way the face of the Son belongs to Mary. It was in her womb that Christ was formed, receiving from her a human resemblance which points to an even greater spiritual closeness. No one has ever devoted himself to the contemplation of the face of Christ as faithfully as Mary. The eyes of her heart already turned to him at the Annunciation, when she conceived him by the power of the Holy Spirit. (*RVM*, 10)

Suggested Resolutions for Today

- *Consider throughout the day Mary's gift of her heart and her total consecration to God.*

- *Resolve to form a life of Marian consecration that boldly enters into Mary's own consecration. This entails knowing Mary's heart, opening your heart to her, and joining her love of Jesus with yours.*

- *Sometime today, pray the Rosary. Focus your attention on Mary's self-giving and the interior movements of her heart.*

Close Your Time of Prayer

With love and devotion in your heart, conclude with the Prayer to Mary for the Second Week.

DAY 21

The Visitation

Begin Your Prayer

Pray the Angelus as an act of presence: Consider the Father's loving gaze upon you, Jesus becoming present to you in Mary, and the Holy Spirit overshadowing you.

Pray for the Light of the Holy Spirit: Pray the Litany of the Holy Spirit with a sense of the Holy Spirit gently penetrating ever deeper into your heart with each invocation.

Form your desire: To feel tremendous joy as you welcome Mary into your heart.

Contemplation

Read slowly and reflectively from Scripture:

> In those days Mary arose and went with haste into the hill country, to a city of Judah, and she entered the house of Zechari'ah and greeted Elizabeth. And when Elizabeth heard the greeting of Mary, the child leaped in her womb; and Elizabeth was filled with the Holy Spirit and she exclaimed with a loud cry, "Blessed are you among women, and blessed is the fruit of your womb! And why is this granted me, that the mother of my Lord should come to me? For behold, when the voice of your greeting came to my ears, the child in my womb leaped for joy. And blessed is she who believed that there would be a fulfilment of what was spoken to her from the Lord." And Mary said,
>
>> "My soul magnifies the Lord,
>> and my spirit rejoices in God my Savior,
>> for he has regarded the low estate of his

handmaiden.

For behold, henceforth all generations will call me
 blessed;
for he who is mighty has done great things for me,
and holy is his name.
And his mercy is on those who fear him
from generation to generation.
He has shown strength with his arm,
he has scattered the proud in the imagination of
 their hearts,
he has put down the mighty from their thrones,
and exalted those of low degree;
he has filled the hungry with good things,
and the rich he has sent empty away.
He has helped his servant Israel,
in remembrance of his mercy,
as he spoke to our fathers,
to Abraham and to his posterity for ever."

And Mary remained with her about three months,
and returned to her home. (Lk 1:39-56)

From Blessed John Paul II:

While every word of Elizabeth's greeting is filled with
meaning, her final words would seem to have fundamental
importance: "And blessed is she who believed that there
would be a fulfillment of what was spoken to her from the
Lord" (Lk 1:45). These words can be linked with the title
"full of grace" of the angel's greeting. Both of these texts
reveal an essential Mariological content, namely, the truth
about Mary, who has become really present in the mystery
of Christ precisely because she "has believed."

The fullness of grace announced by the angel means
the gift of God himself. Mary's faith, proclaimed by
Elizabeth at the Visitation, indicates how the Virgin of
Nazareth responded to this gift. (*RM*, 12)

- *Return to the words and phrases to which you are most
 drawn by the Lord. Ponder them reflectively.*

- *Pray from your heart, conversing with the Father, Jesus, the Holy Spirit, and/or Mary.*

- *Pause and receive from God in some time of silent prayer.*

Resolutions for Forming a Life of Marian Consecration

When Elizabeth heard Mary's greeting she was "filled with the Holy Spirit." Just so, the Holy Spirit will recognize Mary in the hearts of those consecrated through her. As we welcome Mary into our hearts as Elizabeth welcomed Mary into her home, we can expect that the Holy Spirit will stir in our hearts; that Mary will bring us Our Lord; and that she will echo her song of thanksgiving and praise in our lives. Through our consecration Mary shares her blessedness with us. This gift comes through faith as John Paul II explains:

> In proclaiming her "blessed among women", Elizabeth points to Mary's faith as the reason for her blessedness: "And blessed is she who believed that there would be a fulfillment of what was spoken to her from the Lord" (Lk 1:45). Mary's greatness and joy arise from the fact the she is the one who believes. (*Gen. Aud.*, October 2, 1996)

Suggested Resolutions for Today

- *Take account of the blessings God has bestowed upon you in your life. Give thanks to God in your own way, or perhaps with Mary by praying the Magnificat.*

- *Resolve to form a life of Marian consecration that shares Mary's blessedness by immersing your faith in hers.*

- *Sometime today, pray the Rosary. With each mystery welcome Jesus and Mary into your heart.*

Close Your Time of Prayer

With love and devotion in your heart, conclude with the Prayer to Mary for the Second Week.

DAY 22

The Birth
of Jesus

Begin Your Prayer

Pray the Angelus as an act of presence: Consider the Father's loving gaze upon you, Jesus becoming present to you in Mary, and the Holy Spirit overshadowing you.

Pray for the Light of the Holy Spirit: Pray the Litany of the Holy Spirit with a sense of the Holy Spirit gently penetrating ever deeper into your heart with each invocation.

Form your desire: To experience a new gratitude — and even healing — as you ponder Christ's birth.

Contemplation

Read slowly and reflectively from Scripture:

In those days a decree went out from Caesar Augustus that all the world should be enrolled. This was the first enrollment, when Quirin'ius was governor of Syria. And all went to be enrolled, each to his own city. And Joseph also went up from Galilee, from the city of Nazareth, to Judea, to the city of David, which is called Bethlehem, because he was of the house and lineage of David, to be enrolled with Mary, his betrothed, who was with child. And while they were there, the time came for her to be delivered. And she gave birth to her first-born son and wrapped him in swaddling cloths, and laid him in a manger, because there was no place for them in the inn.

And in that region there were shepherds out in the field, keeping watch over their flock by night. And an angel of the Lord appeared to them, and the glory of the Lord shone around them, and they were filled with fear. And the angel said to them, "Be not afraid; for behold, I bring you good news of a great joy which will come to all the people; for to you is born this day in the city of David a Savior, who is Christ the Lord. And this will be a sign for you: you will find a babe wrapped in swaddling cloths and lying in a manger." And suddenly there was with the angel a multitude of the heavenly host praising God and saying,

> "Glory to God in the highest,
> and on earth peace among men with whom he is pleased!"

When the angels went away from them into heaven, the shepherds said to one another, "Let us go over to Bethlehem and see this thing that has happened, which the Lord has made known to us." And they went with haste, and found Mary and Joseph, and the baby lying in a manger. And when they saw it they made known the saying which had been told them concerning this child; and all who heard it wondered at what the shepherds told them. But Mary kept all these things, pondering them in her heart. (Lk 2:1-19)

From Blessed John Paul II:

The description of the birth, recounted in simple fashion, presents Mary as intensely participating in what was taking place in her: "She gave birth to her first-born son and wrapped him in swaddling clothes, and laid him in a manger ..." (Lk 2:7). The Virgin's action is the result of her complete willingness to cooperate in God's plan, already expressed at the Annunciation in her "let it be to me according to your word" (Lk 1:38).

Mary experiences childbirth in a condition of extreme poverty: she cannot give the Son of God even what mothers usually offer a newborn baby; instead, she has to lay him "in a manger," an improvised cradle which contrasts with the dignity of the "Son of the Most High."

The Gospel notes that "there was no place for them in the inn" (Lk 2:7). This statement, recalling the text in John's prologue: "His own people received him not" (Jn 1:11), foretells as it were the many refusals Jesus will meet with during his earthly life. The phrase "for them" joins the Son and the Mother in this rejection, and shows how Mary is already associated with her Son's destiny of suffering and shares in his redeeming mission.

Rejected by "his own," Jesus is welcomed by the shepherds, rough men of ill repute, but chosen by God as the first to receive the good news of the Savior's birth. The message the angel gives them is an invitation to rejoice: "Behold, I bring you good news of a great joy which will come to all the people" (Lk 2:10), along with a request to overcome all fear: "Be not afraid"....

With regard to these extraordinary events, Luke tells us that Mary "kept all these things, pondering them in her heart" (Lk 2:19). While the shepherds passed from fear to wonder and praise, the Virgin, because of her faith, kept alive the memory of the events involving her Son, and deepened her understanding of them by reflecting on them in her heart, that is, in the inmost core of her person. (*Gen. Aud.*, November 20, 1996).

- *Return to the words and phrases to which you are most drawn by the Lord. Ponder them reflectively.*

- *Pray from your heart, conversing with the Father, Jesus, the Holy Spirit, and/or Mary.*

- *Pause and receive from God in some time of silent prayer.*

Resolutions for Forming a Life of Marian Consecration

Through Marian consecration we *remember Christ with Mary*. Blessed John Paul II says that "Mary's contemplation is above all a remembering" (*RVM*, 11). Although we are contemplating life events of Jesus from two thousand years ago, they can bring to us *today* a spiritual relevance, effectiveness, and potency. As we remember these events with Mary, Christ is, in a sense, continually being reborn in us. John Paul II describes Mary's remembering in his teaching on the Rosary:

> Mary lived with her eyes fixed on Christ, treasuring his every word: "She kept all these things, pondering them in her heart" (Lk 2:19; cf. 2:51). The memories of Jesus, impressed upon her heart, were always with her, leading her to reflect on the various moments of her life at her Son's side. In a way those memories were to be the "rosary" which she recited uninterruptedly throughout her earthly life....
>
> Mary constantly sets before the faithful the "mysteries" of her Son, with the desire that the contemplation of those mysteries will release all their saving power. In the recitation of the Rosary, the Christian community enters into contact with the memories and the contemplative gaze of Mary. (*RVM*, 11)

Suggested Resolutions for Today

- *Take a moment to consider the most significant memories of your own life, both the cherished and difficult ones. Invite Jesus and Mary into these memories. Speak to them from your heart.*

- *Resolve to form a life of Marian consecration that actively ponders the saving mysteries of Christ through such means as praying with Scripture and contemplating the mysteries of the Rosary.*

- *Sometime today, pray the Rosary. Unite your prayer to the pondering in Mary's heart.*

Close Your Time of Prayer

With love and devotion in your heart, conclude with the Prayer to Mary for the Second Week.

DAY 23

The Presentation in the Temple

Begin Your Prayer

Pray the Angelus as an act of presence: Consider the Father's loving gaze upon you, Jesus becoming present to you in Mary, and the Holy Spirit overshadowing you.

Pray for the Light of the Holy Spirit: Pray the Litany of the Holy Spirit with a sense of the Holy Spirit gently penetrating ever deeper into your heart with each invocation.

Form your desire: To experience the vulnerability of love as Mary hears the prophecy told of her son and the piercing of her own heart.

Contemplation

Read slowly and reflectively from Scripture:

And when the time came for their purification according to the law of Moses, they brought him up to Jerusalem to present him to the Lord (as it is written in the law of the Lord, "Every male that opens the womb shall be called holy to the Lord") and to offer a sacrifice according to what is said in the law of the Lord, "a pair of turtledoves, or two young pigeons." Now there was a man in Jerusalem, whose name was Simeon, and this man was righteous and devout, looking for the consolation of Israel, and the Holy Spirit was upon him. And it had been revealed to him by the Holy Spirit that he should not see death before he had seen the Lord's Christ. And inspired by the Spirit he came into the temple; and when the parents brought in the child

Jesus, to do for him according to the custom of the law, he took him up in his arms and blessed God and said,

> "Lord, now let your servant depart in peace,
> according to your word;
> for my eyes have seen your salvation
> which you have prepared in the presence of all peoples,
> a light for revelation to the Gentiles,
> and for glory to your people Israel."

And his father and his mother marveled at what was said about him; and Simeon blessed them and said to Mary his mother,

> "Behold, this child is set for the fall and rising of
> many in Israel,
> and for a sign that is spoken against
> (and a sword will pierce through your own soul also),
> that thoughts out of many hearts may be revealed."

And there was a prophetess, Anna, the daughter of Phan'uel, of the tribe of Asher; she was of a great age, having lived with her husband seven years from her virginity, and as a widow till she was eighty-four. She did not depart from the temple, worshiping with fasting and prayer night and day. And coming up at that very hour she gave thanks to God, and spoke of him to all who were looking for the redemption of Jerusalem.

And when they had performed everything according to the law of the Lord, they returned into Galilee, to their own city, Nazareth. And the child grew and became strong, filled with wisdom; and the favor of God was upon him. (Lk 2:22-40)

From Blessed John Paul II:

Turning to the Lord, [Simeon] says: "For my eyes have seen your salvation which you have prepared in the presence of all peoples, a light for revelation to the Gentiles, and for glory to your people Israel" (Lk 2:30-32). At the same time, however, Simeon addresses Mary with the following words: "Behold, this child is set for the fall and rising of many in Israel, and for a sign that is spoken against, that thoughts out of many hearts may be revealed"; and he adds with direct reference to her: "and a sword will pierce through your own soul also" (cf. Lk 2:34-35).

Simeon's words cast new light on the announcement which Mary had heard from the angel: Jesus is the Savior, he is "a light for revelation" to mankind. Is not this what was manifested in a way on Christmas night, when the shepherds come to the stable (cf. Lk 2:8-20)? Is not this what was to be manifested even more clearly in the coming of the Magi from the East (cf. Mt 2:1-12)? But at the same time, at the very beginning of his life, the Son of Mary, and his Mother with him, will experience in themselves the truth of those other words of Simeon: "a sign that is spoken against" (Lk 2:34).

Simeon's words seem like a second annunciation to Mary, for they tell her of the actual historical situation in which the Son is to accomplish his mission, namely, in misunderstanding and sorrow. While this announcement on the one hand confirms her faith in the accomplishment of the divine promises of salvation, on the other hand it also reveals to her that she will have to live her obedience of faith in suffering, at the side of the suffering Savior, and that her motherhood will be mysterious and sorrowful. (*RM*, 16)

- *Return to the words and phrases to which you are most drawn by the Lord. Ponder them reflectively.*

- *Pray from your heart, conversing with the Father, Jesus, the Holy Spirit, and/or Mary.*

- *Pause and receive from God in some time of silent prayer.*

Resolutions for Forming a Life of Marian Consecration

Through Marian consecration we are drawn into the communion of the hearts of Jesus and Mary. Mary has a unique relationship with Jesus as his mother. And yet recognizing that he is the incarnate Son of God, she also makes herself his disciple and unites herself to the intentions of his heart. Jesus and Mary not only share the affection of mother and son, but the oneness of communion. Mary's heart is so united to that of Christ that she will also share in his suffering as is foretold by the prophet Simeon at the presentation of Jesus in the Temple. John Paul II referred to this union as an *alliance of hearts*:

> When the side of Christ was pierced by the centurion's lance it fulfilled Simeon's prophecy to Mary: "And you yourself a sword shall pierce" (Lk 2:35). The words of the prophet are an announcement of the definitive alliance of the hearts of the Son and of the Mother, of the Mother and of the Son. (*Gen. Aud.*, September 15, 1985)

Suggested Resolutions for Today

- *Examine your own life. Are there any intentions or desires of your heart that are contrary to those of Jesus and Mary?*

- *Resolve to form a life of Marian consecration that is in communion with the hearts of Jesus and Mary.*

- *Sometime today pray the Rosary. Be attentive to contemplating the hearts of Jesus and Mary.*

Close Your Time of Prayer

With love and devotion in your heart, conclude with the Prayer to Mary for the Second Week.

DAY 24

Finding Jesus in the Temple

Begin Your Prayer

Pray the Angelus as an act of presence: Consider the Father's loving gaze upon you, Jesus becoming present to you in Mary, and the Holy Spirit overshadowing you.

Pray for the Light of the Holy Spirit: Pray the Litany of the Holy Spirit with a sense of the Holy Spirit gently penetrating ever deeper into your heart with each invocation.

Form your desire: To experience awe and wonder as you learn from and listen to Christ.

Contemplation

Read slowly and reflectively from Scripture:

Now his parents went to Jerusalem every year at the feast of the Passover. And when he was twelve years old, they went up according to custom; and when the feast was ended, as they were returning, the boy Jesus stayed behind in Jerusalem. His parents did not know it, but supposing him to be in the company they went a day's journey, and they sought him among their kinsfolk and acquaintances; and when they did not find him, they returned to Jerusalem, seeking him.

After three days they found him in the temple, sitting among the teachers, listening to them and asking them questions; and all who heard him were amazed at his understanding and his answers. And when they saw him they were astonished; and his mother said to him,

"Son, why have you treated us so? Behold, your father and I have been looking for you anxiously." And he said to them, "How is it that you sought me? Did you not know that I must be in my Father's house?" And they did not understand the saying which he spoke to them. And he went down with them and came to Nazareth, and was obedient to them; and his mother kept all these things in her heart.

And Jesus increased in wisdom and in stature, and in favor with God and man. (Lk 2:41-52)

From Blessed John Paul II:

Joy mixed with drama marks the fifth mystery, the finding of the twelve-year-old Jesus in the Temple. Here he appears in his divine wisdom as he listens and raises questions, already in effect one who "teaches." The revelation of his mystery as the Son wholly dedicated to his Father's affairs proclaims the radical nature of the Gospel, in which even the closest of human relationships are challenged by the absolute demands of the Kingdom. Mary and Joseph, fearful and anxious, "did not understand" his words (Lk 2:50).

To meditate upon the "joyful" mysteries, then, is to enter into the ultimate causes and the deepest meaning of Christian joy. It is to focus on the realism of the mystery of the Incarnation and on the obscure foreshadowing of the mystery of the saving Passion.

Mary leads us to discover the secret of Christian joy, reminding us that Christianity is, first and foremost, *evangelion*, "good news," which has as its heart and its whole content the person of Jesus Christ, the Word made flesh, the one Savior of the world. (*RVM*, 20)

- *Return to the words and phrases to which you are most drawn by the Lord. Ponder them reflectively.*

- *Pray from your heart, conversing with the Father, Jesus, the Holy Spirit, and/or Mary.*

- *Pause and receive from God in some time of silent prayer.*

Resolutions for Forming a Life of Marian Consecration

Through Marian consecration we learn Christ from Mary. To be a disciple of Jesus means to learn his truth, his values, and his way of love. Sometimes, we have to unlearn what we have learned or undo certain habits in order to faithfully respond to his truth. Mary helps us to learn Christ. She helps us to cultivate new habits and virtues. Blessed John Paul II speaks of learning Christ in his teaching on the Rosary:

> Christ is the supreme Teacher, the revealer and the one revealed. It is not just a question of learning what he taught but of *"learning him."* In this regard could we have any better teacher than Mary? From the divine standpoint, the Spirit is the interior teacher who leads us to the full truth of Christ. But among creatures no one knows Christ better than Mary; no one can introduce us to a profound knowledge of his mystery better than his Mother. (*RVM*, 14)

Suggested Resolutions for Today

- *Consider your new life of consecration to be a School of Mary. Seek to foster an eagerness to learn Christ in contemplating him with Mary.*

- *Sometime today, pray the Rosary. As a disciple seek to learn from each mystery.*

Close Your Time of Prayer

With love and devotion in your heart, conclude with the Prayer to Mary for the Second Week.

DAY 25

The Wedding at Cana

Begin Your Prayer

Pray the Angelus as an act of presence: Consider the Father's loving gaze upon you, Jesus becoming present to you in Mary, and the Holy Spirit overshadowing you.

Pray for the Light of the Holy Spirit: Pray the Litany of the Holy Spirit with a sense of the Holy Spirit gently penetrating ever deeper into your heart with each invocation.

Form your desire: To experience great confidence with the knowledge of Mary's prayer for you.

Contemplation

Read slowly and reflectively from Scripture:

On the third day there was a marriage at Cana in Galilee, and the mother of Jesus was there; Jesus also was invited to the marriage, with his disciples. When the wine failed, the mother of Jesus said to him, "They have no wine." And Jesus said to her, "O woman, what have you to do with me? My hour has not yet come." His mother said to the servants, "Do whatever he tells you." Now six stone jars were standing there, for the Jewish rites of purification, each holding twenty or thirty gallons. Jesus said to them, "Fill the jars with water." And they filled them up to the brim. He said to them, "Now draw some out, and take it to the steward of the feast." So they took it. When the steward of the feast tasted the water now become wine, and did not know where it came from (though the servants who had drawn the water knew), the steward of the feast called the bridegroom and said to him, "Every man serves the good wine first; and when men have drunk freely, then the poor wine; but you have kept the good wine until now." This, the first of his signs, Jesus did at Cana in Galilee, and manifested his glory; and his disciples believed in him. (Jn 2:1-11)

From Blessed John Paul II:

What deep understanding existed between Jesus and his mother? How can we probe the mystery of their intimate spiritual union? ... The description of the Cana event outlines what is actually manifested as a new kind of motherhood according to the spirit and not just according to the flesh, that is to say Mary's solicitude for human beings, her coming to them in the wide variety of their wants and needs. At Cana in Galilee there is shown only one concrete aspect of human need, apparently a small one of little importance ("They have no wine"). But it has a symbolic value: this coming to the aid of human needs means, at the same time, bringing those needs within the radius of Christ's messianic mission and salvific power.

Thus there is a mediation: Mary places herself between her Son and mankind in the reality of their wants, needs and sufferings. She puts herself "in the middle," that is to say she acts as a mediatrix not as an outsider, but in her position as mother. She knows that as such she can point out to her Son the needs of mankind, and, in fact, she "has the right" to do so. Her mediation is thus in the nature of intercession: Mary "intercedes" for mankind.

And that is not all. As a mother she also wishes the messianic power of her Son to be manifested, that salvific power of his which is meant to help man in his misfortunes, to free him from the evil which in various forms and degrees weighs heavily upon his life....

Another essential element of Mary's maternal task is found in her words to the servants: "Do whatever he tells you." The Mother of Christ presents herself as the spokeswoman of her Son's will, pointing out those things which must be done so that the salvific power of the Messiah may be manifested. At Cana, thanks to the intercession of Mary and the obedience of the servants, Jesus begins "his hour." At Cana Mary appears as believing in Jesus. Her faith evokes his first "sign" and helps to kindle the faith of the disciples. (*RM*, 21)

- *Return to the words and phrases to which you are most drawn by the Lord. Ponder them reflectively.*

- *Pray from your heart, conversing with the Father, Jesus, the Holy Spirit, and/or Mary.*

- *Pause and receive from God in some time of silent prayer.*

Resolutions for Forming a Life of Marian Consecration

Through Marian consecration we pray to Christ with Mary. At the wedding in Cana Jesus performs his first public miracle through the intercession of Mary — the miracle by which his disciples begin to believe in him. Mary intercedes for us with the concern of a mother. What great confidence we feel knowing that Mary prays for us! Blessed John Paul II speaks of the powerful role of Mary's intercession in his teaching on the Rosary:

> In support of the prayer which Christ and the Spirit cause to rise in our hearts, Mary intervenes with her maternal intercession. . . . At the wedding of Cana the Gospel clearly shows the power of Mary's intercession as she makes known to Jesus the needs of others: "They have no wine" (Jn 2:3). (*RVM*, 16)

Suggested Resolutions for Today

- *Consider Mary's constancy toward you. Cultivate an awareness of her praying for you and with you as you pray to God.*

- *Sometime today, pray the Rosary. Be attentive to contemplating the mysteries of the Rosary as you pray to Jesus with Mary.*

Close Your Time of Prayer

With love and devotion in your heart, conclude with the Prayer to Mary for the Second Week.

DAY 26

At the Foot of the Cross

Begin Your Prayer

Pray the Angelus as an act of presence: Consider the Father's loving gaze upon you, Jesus becoming present to you in Mary, and the Holy Spirit overshadowing you.

Pray for the Light of the Holy Spirit: Pray the Litany of the Holy Spirit with a sense of the Holy Spirit gently penetrating ever deeper into your heart with each invocation.

Form your desire: To humbly acknowledge the gift that Jesus gives you from the cross — Mary as your Mother.

Contemplation

Read slowly and reflectively from Scripture:

> But standing by the cross of Jesus were his mother, and his mother's sister, Mary the wife of Clopas, and Mary Mag'dalene. When Jesus saw his mother, and the disciple whom he loved standing near, he said to his mother, "Woman, behold, your son!" Then he said to the disciple, "Behold, your mother!" And from that hour the disciple took her to his own home.
> After this Jesus, knowing that all was now finished, said (to fulfil the Scripture), "I thirst." A bowl full of vinegar stood there; so they put a sponge full of the vinegar on hyssop and held it to his mouth. When Jesus had received

the vinegar, he said, "It is finished"; and he bowed his head and gave up his spirit. (Jn 19:25-30)

From Blessed John Paul II:

The Redeemer entrusts Mary to John because he entrusts John to Mary. At the foot of the Cross there begins that special entrusting of humanity to the Mother of Christ, which in the history of the Church has been practiced and expressed in different ways.

The same Apostle and Evangelist, after reporting the words addressed by Jesus on the Cross to his Mother and to himself, adds: "And from that hour the disciple took her to his own home" (Jn 19:27). This statement certainly means that the role of son was attributed to the disciple and that he assumed responsibility for the Mother of his beloved Master.

And since Mary was given as a mother to him personally, the statement indicates, even though indirectly, everything expressed by the intimate relationship of a child with its mother. And all of this can be included in the word "entrusting." Such entrusting is the response to a person's love, and in particular to the love of a mother.

The Marian dimension of the life of a disciple of Christ is expressed in a special way precisely through this filial entrusting to the Mother of Christ, which began with the testament of the Redeemer on Golgotha. Entrusting himself to Mary in a filial manner, the Christian, like the Apostle John, "welcomes" the Mother of Christ "into his own home" and brings her into everything that makes up his inner life, that is to say into his human and Christian "I": he "took her to his own home." (*RM*, 45)

- *Return to the words and phrases to which you are most drawn by the Lord. Ponder them reflectively.*

- *Pray from your heart, conversing with the Father, Jesus, the Holy Spirit, and/or Mary.*

- *Pause and receive from God in some time of silent prayer.*

Resolutions for Forming a Life of Marian Consecration

Blessed John Paul II considers Marian consecration to be a filial entrustment to the Mother of Christ. At the foot of the Cross, Jesus gives Mary as a gift which Christ himself makes personally to every individual. As John took Mary into his own home so are we to take Mary into our own inner life.

> On the cross Jesus did not proclaim Mary's universal motherhood formally, but established a concrete maternal relationship between her and the beloved disciple. In the Lord's choice we can see his concern that this motherhood should not be interpreted in a vague way, but should point to Mary's intense, personal relationship with individual Christians. May each one of us, precisely through the concrete reality of Mary's universal motherhood, fully acknowledge her as our own Mother, and trustingly commend ourselves to her maternal love. (*Gen. Aud.*, April 23, 1997)

Suggested Resolutions for Today

- *Review the past week. Consider for yourself what have been the most significant graces that you have received or perhaps the areas that may still challenge you. Converse lovingly with Mary about these areas. Summarize these in your journal.*

- *Sometime today, pray the Rosary.*

Close Your Time of Prayer

With love and devotion in your heart, conclude with the Prayer to Mary for the Second Week.

THIRD WEEK

Knowledge of Jesus

This is the final week of preparation for total consecration. It is devoted to gaining a greater personal knowledge of Jesus Christ. This is what our entire consecration through Mary is directed toward. Continue to foster a sense of Mary beside you as you contemplate Christ during this week. Desire to know him interiorly, contemplating his Sacred Heart. As before, review the steps of prayer for this week. The only difference from the previous week is the concluding prayer to Jesus and the Holy Spirit that is adapted from a prayer written by Saint Louis de Montfort. If you haven't already, take a look ahead at the introduction for the Day of Consecration in order to make the preparations for that day.

PRAYERS TO BE USED DURING THE THIRD WEEK

Angelus

V. The angel of the Lord declared unto Mary.

R. And she conceived by the power of the Holy Spirit.
Hail Mary ...

V. Behold the handmaid of the Lord.

R. Be it done unto me according to your Word.

Hail Mary ...

V. And the Word was made flesh.

R. And dwelt among us.

Hail Mary ...

V. Pray for us, O Holy Mother of God.

R. That we may be made worthy of the promises of Christ.

Let us pray.

Pour forth, we beseech you, O Lord, your grace into our hearts, that we to whom the incarnation of Christ your Son was made known by the message of an angel, may by his Passion and Cross be brought to the glory of his resurrection; through the same Christ our Lord. Amen.

Litany of the Holy Spirit

Lord, *have mercy on us.*
Christ, *have mercy on us.*
Lord, *have mercy on us.*
Father all powerful, *have mercy on us.*
Jesus, Eternal Son of the Father, Redeemer of the world, *save us.*
Spirit of the Father and the Son, boundless life of both, *sanctify us.*
Holy Trinity, *hear us.*

Holy Spirit, who proceeds from the Father and the Son, *enter our hearts.*
Holy Spirit, equal to the Father and the Son, *enter our hearts.*

Promise of God the Father, *have mercy on us.*
Ray of heavenly light ...
Author of all good ...
Source of heavenly water ...
Consuming fire ...

Ardent charity, *have mercy on us.*
Spiritual unction ...
Spirit of love and truth ...
Spirit of wisdom and understanding ...
Spirit of counsel and fortitude ...
Spirit of knowledge and piety ...
Spirit of the fear of the Lord ...
Spirit of grace and prayer ...
Spirit of peace and meekness ...
Spirit of modesty and innocence ...
Holy Spirit, the Comforter ...
Holy Spirit, the Sanctifier ...
Holy Spirit, who governs the Church ...
Gift of God, the Most High ...
Spirit who fills the universe ...
Spirit of the adoption of the children of God ...

Holy Spirit, *inspire us with horror of sin.*
Holy Spirit, *come and renew the face of the earth.*
Holy Spirit, *shed your light in our souls.*
Holy Spirit, *engrave your law in our hearts.*
Holy Spirit, *inflame us with the flame of your love.*
Holy Spirit, *open to us the treasures of your graces.*
Holy Spirit, *teach us to pray well.*
Holy Spirit, *enlighten us with your heavenly inspirations.*
Holy Spirit, *lead us in the way of salvation.*
Holy Spirit, *grant us the only necessary knowledge.*
Holy Spirit, *inspire in us the practice of good.*
Holy Spirit, *grant us the merits of all virtues.*
Holy Spirit, *make us persevere in justice.*
Holy Spirit, *be our everlasting reward.*

Lamb of God, who takes away the sins of the world,
    Send us your Holy Spirit.

Lamb of God, who takes away the sins of the world,
    Pour down into our souls the gifts of the Holy Spirit.

Lamb of God, who takes away the sins of the world,

Grant us the Spirit of wisdom and piety.

V. Come, Holy Spirit! Fill the hearts of your faithful,
R. *And enkindle in them the fire of your love.*

Let us pray. Grant, O merciful Father, that your Divine Spirit may enlighten, inflame and purify us, that He may penetrate us with His heavenly dew and make us fruitful in good works, through Our Lord Jesus Christ, your Son, who with you, in the unity of the same Spirit, lives and reigns forever and ever. Amen.

Prayer to Jesus and the Holy Spirit for the Third Week

O most loving Jesus, I give you thanks that in spite of my unworthiness you invite me to entrust myself totally to Mary your Mother, she who gives herself fully to her spiritual sons and daughters. In response to her gift of self, may I, in turn, give myself entirely to her, and thus to you with her.

Mary is in me! What a treasure, what a consolation. May I be entirely hers. With Saint John the Beloved Disciple at the foot of the cross, I have taken her many times for my own and have given myself to her. But if I have not done this as you, dear Jesus, desire, I now renew this offering. If you see in my soul or body anything that does not belong to her, take it and cast it far away from me for whatever in me does not belong to Mary is not worthy of you.

O Holy Spirit, plant in my soul the tree of true life, which is Mary. Cultivate it and tend it so that it may grow and blossom and bring forth the fruit of life in abundance. O Holy Spirit, give me great devotion to Mary, your faithful spouse; give me great confidence in her maternal heart and an abiding refuge in her steadfast love, so that by her you may truly form Jesus Christ in me. Amen.

DAY 27

Proclamation of the Kingdom

Begin Your Prayer

Pray the Angelus as an act of presence: Consider the Father's loving gaze upon you, Jesus becoming present to you in Mary, and the Holy Spirit overshadowing you.

Pray for the Light of the Holy Spirit: Pray the Litany of the Holy Spirit with a sense of the Holy Spirit gently penetrating ever deeper into your heart with each invocation.

Form your desire: A renewed desire and readiness to welcome Christ and his Good News.

Contemplation

Read slowly and reflectively from Scripture:

Now after John was arrested, Jesus came into Galilee, preaching the gospel of God, and saying, "The time is fulfilled, and the kingdom of God is at hand; repent, and believe in the gospel." (Mk 1:14-15)

And he came to Nazareth, where he had been brought up; and he went to the synagogue, as was his custom, on the sabbath day. And he stood up to read; and there was given to him the book of the prophet Isaiah. He opened the book and found the place where it was written,

"The Spirit of the Lord is upon me,
because he has anointed me to preach good news to the poor.
He has sent me to proclaim release to the captives

and recovering of sight to the blind,
to set at liberty those who are oppressed,
to proclaim the acceptable year of the Lord."

And he closed the book, and gave it back to the attendant, and sat down; and the eyes of all in the synagogue were fixed on him. And he began to say to them, "Today this scripture has been fulfilled in your hearing." And all spoke well of him, and wondered at the gracious words which proceeded out of his mouth; and they said, "Is not this Joseph's son?" (Lk 4:16-22)

From Blessed John Paul II:

Jesus of Nazareth brings God's plan to fulfillment. After receiving the Holy Spirit at his baptism, Jesus makes clear his messianic calling: he goes about Galilee "preaching the Gospel of God and saying: 'The time is fulfilled, and the kingdom of God is at hand; repent and believe in the Gospel'" (Mk 1:14-15). The proclamation and establishment of God's kingdom are the purpose of his mission: "I was sent for this purpose" (Lk 4:43).

But that is not all. Jesus himself is the "Good News," as he declares at the very beginning of his mission in the synagogue at Nazareth, when he applies to himself the words of Isaiah about the Anointed One sent by the Spirit of the Lord. Since the "Good News" is Christ, there is an identity between the message and the messenger, between saying, doing and being. His power, the secret of the effectiveness of his actions, lies in his total identification with the message he announces; he proclaims the "Good News" not just by what he says or does, but by what he is. ...

The kingdom which Jesus inaugurates is the kingdom of God. Jesus himself reveals who this God is, the One whom he addresses by the intimate term "Abba," Father. God, as revealed above all in the parables, is sensitive to the needs and sufferings of every human being: he is a Father filled with love and compassion, who grants forgiveness and freely bestows the favors asked of him. Saint John tells us that "God is love" (1 Jn 4:8; 4:16).

Every person therefore is invited to "repent" and to "believe" in God's merciful love. The Kingdom will grow insofar as every person learns to turn to God in the intimacy of prayer as to a Father and strives to do his will. (*MR*, 13)

- *Return to the words and phrases to which you are most drawn by the Lord. Ponder them reflectively.*

- *Pray from your heart, conversing with the Father, Jesus, the Holy Spirit, and/or Mary.*

- *Pause and receive from God in some time of silent prayer.*

Resolutions for Forming a Life of Marian Consecration

The words of John Paul II from his inaugural papal Mass bear repeating as we begin the third week: "Do not be afraid! Open, indeed, open wide the doors to Christ!" Jesus is the Good News himself. Through your consecration, you are opening the doors to him. If you have any hesitancy about moving forward or are doubtful whether you have prepared sufficiently, now is the time to lay those concerns aside and let Christ come to you through Mary. His kingdom — his love, his reign, his peace, his freedom — awaits you. Redetermine to welcome Christ with eager expectation in this final week. Desire to know him and to contemplate his face.

Do not be afraid. Christ knows "what is in man." He alone knows it.

So often today man does not know what is within him, in the depths of his mind and heart. So often he is uncertain about the meaning of his life on this earth. He is assailed by doubt, a doubt which turns into despair. We ask you therefore, we beg you with humility and trust, let

Christ speak to man. He alone has words of life, yes, of eternal life. (*Homily*, October 22, 1978)

Suggested Resolutions for Today

- *Resolve to form a life of Marian consecration that seeks to grow in knowledge and love of Christ through Sacred Scripture. Consider adopting a routine of praying with Scripture as your new life begins.*

- *Prepare to receive the Sacrament of Reconciliation sometime this week prior to your consecration.*

- *Sometime today, pray the Rosary.*

Close Your Time of Prayer

With joyful anticipation of your approaching consecration, pray the Prayer to Jesus and the Holy Spirit for the Third Week.

DAY 28

Call of the Disciples

Begin Your Prayer

Pray the Angelus as an act of presence: Consider the Father's loving gaze upon you, Jesus becoming present to you in Mary, and the Holy Spirit overshadowing you.

Pray for the Light of the Holy Spirit: Pray the Litany of the Holy Spirit with a sense of the Holy Spirit gently penetrating ever deeper into your heart with each invocation.

Form your desire: A longing to stay with the Lord.

Contemplation

Read slowly and reflectively from Scripture:

The next day again John was standing with two of his disciples; and he looked at Jesus as he walked, and said, "Behold, the Lamb of God!" The two disciples heard him say this, and they followed Jesus. Jesus turned, and saw them following, and said to them, "What do you seek?" And they said to him, "Rabbi" (which means Teacher), "where are you staying?" He said to them, "Come and see." They came and saw where he was staying; and they stayed with him that day, for it was about the tenth hour. One of the two who heard John speak, and followed him, was Andrew, Simon Peter's brother. He first found his brother Simon, and said to him, "We have found the Messiah" (which means Christ). (Jn 1:35-41)

From Blessed John Paul II:

It is along the paths of daily life that you can meet the Lord! Do you remember how the disciples, hurrying to the banks of the Jordan to listen to the last of the great prophets, John the Baptist, saw Jesus of Nazareth pointed out to them as the Messiah, the Lamb of God? Out of curiosity they decided to follow him at a distance. They were shy almost and embarrassed, until, turning round, he asked them: "What do you seek?" So began the dialogue that would give rise to the adventure of John, Andrew, Simon "Peter" and the other apostles (cf. Jn 1:29-51).

In this concrete and surprising encounter, described in a few, essential words, we find the origin of every journey in faith. It is Jesus who takes the initiative. When we have to do with him, the question is always turned upside down: from questioners, we become questioned; "searchers," we discover that we are "sought"; he, indeed, has always loved us first (cf. 1 Jn 4:10).

This is the fundamental dimension of the encounter: we are not dealing with something, but with Someone, with the "Living One." (*Message for World Youth Day XII*, 1996)

- *Return to the words and phrases to which you are most drawn by the Lord. Ponder them reflectively.*

- *Pray from your heart, conversing with the Father, Jesus, the Holy Spirit, and/or Mary.*

- *Pause and receive from God in some time of silent prayer.*

Resolutions for Forming a Life of Marian Consecration

Whether we know it or not, each of us is on a quest seeking God. We often try to fill our inner longing with created things, but eventually find them to be unsatisfying and passing. Ultimately, our hearts are made for God. Jesus, who is the fulfillment of all desire, is already seeking us. He *stayed* with Mary for much of his life. In a life of consecration, Mary will draw us into the encounter with him and invite us to where the Lord is *staying*. Blessed John Paul II said to young people:

> Like the first disciples, follow Jesus! Do not be afraid to draw near to him, to cross the threshold of his dwelling, to speak with him face to face, as you talk with a friend. Do not be afraid of the "new life" he is offering. He himself makes it possible for you to receive that Life and practice it, with the help of his grace and the gift of his Spirit....
>
> Recognizing that you are "new" men and women regenerated by the grace of baptism, talk with Jesus in prayer and while listening to the Word; experience the joy of reconciliation in the Sacrament of Penance, receive the Body and Blood of Christ in the Eucharist, welcome and serve him in your brothers and sisters. You will discover the truth about yourselves and your inner unity, and you will find a "Thou" who gives the cure for anxieties, for nightmares, and for the unbridled subjectivism that leaves you no peace. (*Message for World Youth Day XII*, 1996)

Suggested Resolutions for Today

- *Resolve to form a life of Marian consecration that stays with the Lord in prayer, the sacraments, and service to others. Examine your commitments in these areas. With generosity, consider any new resolutions you might like to make for your new life of consecration.*

- *Sometime today, pray the Rosary.*

Close Your Time of Prayer

With joyful anticipation of your approaching consecration, pray the Prayer to Jesus and the Holy Spirit for the Third Week.

DAY 29

Take Up
Your Cross

Begin Your Prayer

Pray the Angelus as an act of presence: Consider the Father's loving gaze upon you, Jesus becoming present to you in Mary, and the Holy Spirit overshadowing you.

Pray for the Light of the Holy Spirit: Pray the Litany of the Holy Spirit with a sense of the Holy Spirit gently penetrating ever deeper into your heart with each invocation.

Form your desire: Courage to take up your cross and follow the Lord.

Contemplation

Read slowly and reflectively from Scripture:

And he said to all, "If any man would come after me, let him deny himself and take up his cross daily and follow me. For whoever would save his life will lose it; and whoever loses his life for my sake, he will save it. For what does it profit a man if he gains the whole world and loses or forfeits himself?" (Lk 9:23-25)

From Blessed John Paul II:

I invite you to reflect on the conditions that Jesus asked of those who wanted to be his disciples: "If anyone wishes to come after me", he said, "he must deny himself and take up his cross daily and follow me" (Lk 9:23). Jesus is not a

Messiah of triumph and power. In fact, he did not free Israel from Roman rule and he never assured it of political glory. As a true Servant of the Lord, he carried out his mission in solidarity, in service, and in the humiliation of death. He is the Messiah who did not fit into any mold and who came without fanfare, and who cannot be "understood" with the logic of success and power, the kind of logic often used by the world to verify its projects and actions.

Having come to carry out the will of the Father, Jesus remained faithful to it right to the end. He thus carried out his mission of salvation for all those who believe in him and love him, not in word, but in deed. Love is the condition for following him, but it is sacrifice that is the proof of that love. "If anyone wishes to come after me, let him deny himself and take up his cross daily and follow me" (Lk 9:23). These words denote the radicality of a choice that does not allow for hesitation or second thoughts. It is a demanding requirement that unsettled even the disciples and that, throughout the ages, has held back many men and women from following Christ.

But precisely this radicality has also produced admirable examples of sanctity and martyrdom that strengthened and confirmed the way of the Church. Even today these words are regarded as a stumbling block and folly. Yet they must be faced, because the path outlined by God for his Son is the path to be undertaken by the disciple who has decided to follow Jesus. There are not two paths, but only one: the one trodden by the Master. The disciple cannot invent a different way. (*Message for World Youth Day XVI*, 2001)

- *Return to the words and phrases to which you are most drawn by the Lord. Ponder them reflectively.*

- *Pray from your heart, conversing with the Father, Jesus, the Holy Spirit, and/or Mary.*

- *Pause and receive from God in some time of silent prayer.*

Resolutions for Forming a Life of Marian Consecration

The condition for following Christ is love — a love that is capable of sacrifice. A life of consecration to Jesus through Mary, by your communion with them, will lead you along this same path of love: to deny yourself and take up your cross. Blessed John Paul II reiterates how this is for the sake of love:

> "Take up his cross daily and follow me." As the cross can be reduced to being an ornament, "to carry the cross" can become just a manner of speaking. In the teaching of Jesus, however, it does not imply the preeminence of mortification and denial. It does not refer primarily to the need to endure patiently the great and small tribulations of life, or, even less, to the exaltation of pain as a means of pleasing God. It is not suffering for its own sake that a Christian seeks, but love. When the cross is embraced it becomes a sign of love and of total self-giving. To carry it behind Christ means to be united with him in offering the greatest proof of love. (*Message for World Youth Day XVI*, 2001)

Suggested Resolutions for Today

- *With Mary beside you to strengthen you, consider what it means for you to take up your cross and follow Christ.*

- *Resolve to form a life of Marian consecration by which you are willing to deny yourself, take up your cross daily, and follow the Lord.*

- *Sometime today, pray the Rosary.*

Close Your Time of Prayer

With joyful anticipation of your approaching consecration, pray the Prayer to Jesus and the Holy Spirit for the Third Week.

DAY 30

The Transfiguration

Begin Your Prayer

Pray the Angelus as an act of presence: Consider the Father's loving gaze upon you, Jesus becoming present to you in Mary, and the Holy Spirit overshadowing you.

Pray for the Light of the Holy Spirit: Pray the Litany of the Holy Spirit with a sense of the Holy Spirit gently penetrating ever deeper into your heart with each invocation.

Form your desire: Be encouraged and strengthened by the Transfiguration of Jesus.

Contemplation

Read slowly and reflectively from Scripture:

Now about eight days after these sayings he took with him Peter and John and James, and went up on the mountain to pray. And as he was praying, the appearance of his countenance was altered, and his clothing became dazzling white. And behold, two men talked with him, Moses and Eli'jah, who appeared in glory and spoke of his exodus, which he was to accomplish at Jerusalem. Now Peter and those who were with him were heavy with sleep but kept awake, and they saw his glory and the two men who stood with him. And as the men were parting from him, Peter said to Jesus, "Master, it is well that we are here; let us make three booths, one for you and one for Moses and one for Eli'jah" — not knowing what he said. As he said this, a cloud came and overshadowed them; and they were afraid as they entered the cloud. And a voice came out of the cloud, saying, "This is my Son, my Chosen; listen to him!" And when the voice had spoken, Jesus was found alone. And they kept silence and told no one in those days anything of what they had seen. (Lk 9:28-36)

From Blessed John Paul II:

"And he was transfigured before them, and his face shone like the sun" (Mt 17:2). The Gospel scene of Christ's transfiguration, in which the three apostles Peter, James and John appear entranced by the beauty of the Redeemer, can be seen as an icon of Christian contemplation. To look upon the face of Christ, to recognize its mystery amid the daily events and the sufferings of his human life, and then to grasp the divine splendor definitively revealed in the risen Lord, seated in glory at the right hand of the Father: this is the task of every follower of Christ and therefore the task of each one of us.

In contemplating Christ's face we become open to receiving the mystery of Trinitarian life, experiencing ever anew the love of the Father and delighting in the joy of the Holy Spirit. Saint Paul's words can then be applied to us: "Beholding the glory of the Lord, we are being changed into his likeness, from one degree of glory to another; for this comes from the Lord who is the Spirit" (2 Cor 3:18). (*RVM*, 9)

- *Return to the words and phrases to which you are most drawn by the Lord. Ponder them reflectively.*

- *Pray from your heart, conversing with the Father, Jesus, the Holy Spirit, and/or Mary.*

- *Pause and receive from God in some time of silent prayer.*

Resolutions for Forming a Life of Marian Consecration

In the mystery of the Transfiguration the splendor of Christ's divinity is revealed. Moreover, as "Jesus Christ fully reveals man to himself," we recognize that this mystery points to our own destiny. As the Holy Spirit is present and the Father is delighting in his beloved Son, we too are to be drawn into the communion of the Trinity through a life of holiness. Blessed John Paul II said, "Holiness . . . is the living reflection of the face of Christ" (*NMI*, 7). Saint Louis de Montfort explains that one of the principle effects of our consecration to Jesus through Mary is a *transformation into the likeness of Christ*:

> If Mary, who is the tree of life, is well cultivated in our soul by fidelity to the practices of this devotion, she will bear her fruit in her own time, and her fruit is none other than Jesus Christ. (*TD*, 218)

Suggested Resolutions for Today

- *As Peter, James, and John would later be encouraged during their trials by their memory of the Transfiguration, draw upon the splendor and light of Christ to dispel the darkness of any fear or discouragement you may be experiencing.*

- *Resolve to form a life of Marian consecration illumined by Christ and filled with hope.*

- *Sometime today, pray the Rosary.*

Close Your Time of Prayer

With joyful anticipation of your approaching consecration, pray the Prayer to Jesus and the Holy Spirit for the Third Week.

DAY 31

The Eucharist

Begin Your Prayer

Pray the Angelus as an act of presence: Consider the Father's loving gaze upon you, Jesus becoming present to you in Mary, and the Holy Spirit overshadowing you.

Pray for the Light of the Holy Spirit: Pray the Litany of the Holy Spirit with a sense of the Holy Spirit gently penetrating ever deeper into your heart with each invocation.

Form your desire: A new amazement at Our Lord's presence in the Eucharist.

Contemplation

Read slowly and reflectively from Scripture:

And when the hour came, he sat at table, and the apostles with him. And he said to them, "I have earnestly desired to eat this Passover with you before I suffer; for I tell you I shall not eat it until it is fulfilled in the kingdom of God." And he took a chalice, and when he had given thanks he said, "Take this, and divide it among yourselves; for I tell you that from now on I shall not drink of the fruit of the vine until the kingdom of God comes." And he took bread, and when he had given thanks he broke it and gave it to them, saying, "This is my body which is given for you. Do this in remembrance of me." And likewise the chalice after supper, saying, "This chalice which is poured out for you is the new covenant in my blood." (Lk 22:14-20)

So Jesus said to them, "Truly, truly, I say to you, unless you eat the flesh of the Son of man and drink his blood, you have no life in you; he who eats my flesh and drinks my blood has eternal life, and I will raise him up at the last day. For my flesh is food indeed, and my blood is drink indeed. He who eats my flesh and drinks my blood abides in me, and I in him. (Jn 6:53-56)

From Blessed John Paul II:

The Church has received the Eucharist from Christ her Lord not as one gift — however precious — among so many others, but as the gift par excellence, for it is the gift of himself, of his person in his sacred humanity, as well as the gift of his saving work. Nor does it remain confined to the past, since "all that Christ is — all that he did and suffered for all men — participates in the divine eternity, and so transcends all times" (CCC, n. 1085).

When the Church celebrates the Eucharist, the memorial of her Lord's death and resurrection, this central event of salvation becomes really present and "the work of our redemption is carried out." This sacrifice is so decisive for the salvation of the human race that Jesus Christ offered it and returned to the Father only after he had left us a means of sharing in it as if we had been present there. Each member of the faithful can thus take part in it and inexhaustibly gain its fruits.

This is the faith from which generations of Christians down the ages have lived. The Church's magisterium has constantly reaffirmed this faith with joyful gratitude for its inestimable gift. I wish once more to recall this truth and to join you, my dear brothers and sisters, in adoration before this mystery: a great mystery, a mystery of mercy.

What more could Jesus have done for us? Truly, in the Eucharist, he shows us a love which goes "to the end," a love which knows no measure. (EE, 11)

- *Return to the words and phrases to which you are most drawn by the Lord. Ponder them reflectively.*
- *Pray from your heart, conversing with the Father, Jesus, the Holy Spirit, and/or Mary.*

- *Pause and receive from God in some time of silent prayer.*

Resolutions for Forming a Life of Marian Consecration

The Eucharist is the source and summit of our life as Christians. Blessed John Paul II says that "Mary is a woman of the Eucharist in her whole life" (*EE*, 53). We can turn to Mary in our life of consecration to help us "contemplate the face of Jesus" in this great sacrament — to see Christ's presence with the eyes of faith and to receive him with greater love.

> What must Mary have felt as she heard from the mouth of Peter, John, James, and the other apostles the words spoken at the Last Supper: "This is my body which is given for you" (Lk 22:19)? The body given up for us and made present under sacramental signs was the same body which she had conceived in her womb! For Mary, receiving the Eucharist must have somehow meant welcoming once more into her womb that heart which had beat in unison with hers and reliving what she had experienced at the foot of the Cross. (*EE*, 56)

Suggested Resolutions for Today

- *Saint Louis de Montfort recommended praying to Mary before receiving Communion in order to dispose ourselves to receive Christ. Consider making this your own practice.*

- *Resolve to form a life of Marian consecration that is Eucharistic. Make Sunday Mass a focal point of your week. Try to attend daily Mass as you are able, and make visits to the Blessed Sacrament.*

- *Sometime today, pray the Rosary.*

Close Your Time of Prayer

With joyful anticipation of your approaching consecration, pray the Prayer to Jesus and the Holy Spirit for the Third Week.

DAY 32

The Crucifixion

Begin Your Prayer

Pray the Angelus as an act of presence: Consider the Father's loving gaze upon you, Jesus becoming present to you in Mary, and the Holy Spirit overshadowing you.

Pray for the Light of the Holy Spirit: Pray the Litany of the Holy Spirit with a sense of the Holy Spirit gently penetrating ever deeper into your heart with each invocation.

Form your desire: A humble surrender of all that you are before Jesus on the cross.

Contemplation

Read slowly and reflectively from Scripture:

> And it was the third hour, when they crucified him. And the inscription of the charge against him read, "The King of the Jews." And with him they crucified two robbers, one on his right and one on his left. And those who passed by derided him, shaking their heads, and saying, "Aha! You who would destroy the temple and build it in three days, save yourself, and come down from the cross!" So also the chief priests mocked him to one another with the scribes, saying, "He saved others; he cannot save himself. Let the Christ, the King of Israel, come down now from the cross, that we may see and believe." Those who were crucified with him also reviled him.
>
> And when the sixth hour had come, there was darkness over the whole land until the ninth hour. And at

the ninth hour Jesus cried with a loud voice, "E'lo-i, E'lo-i, la'ma sabach-tha'ni?" which means, "My God, my God, why have you forsaken me?" And some of the bystanders hearing it said, "Behold, he is calling Eli'jah." And one ran and, filling a sponge full of vinegar, put it on a reed and gave it to him to drink, saying, "Wait, let us see whether Eli'jah will come to take him down." And Jesus uttered a loud cry, and breathed his last. And the curtain of the temple was torn in two, from top to bottom. And when the centurion, who stood facing him, saw that he thus breathed his last, he said, "Truly this man was the Son of God!" (Mk 15:25-39)

From Blessed John Paul II:

Suffering, in fact, is always a trial — at times a very hard one — to which humanity is subjected. The Gospel paradox of weakness and strength often speaks to us from the pages of the Letters of Saint Paul, a paradox particularly experienced by the apostle himself and together with him experienced by all who share Christ's sufferings.

Paul writes in the Second Letter to the Corinthians: "I will all the more gladly boast of my weaknesses, that the power of Christ may rest upon me" (12:9). In the Second Letter to Timothy we read: "And therefore I suffer as I do. But I am not ashamed, for I know whom I have believed" (1:12). And in the Letter to the Philippians he will even say: "I can do all things in him who strengthens me" (4:13).

Those who share in Christ's sufferings have before their eyes the Paschal Mystery of the Cross and Resurrection, in which Christ descends, in a first phase, to the ultimate limits of human weakness and impotence: indeed, he dies nailed to the cross. But if at the same time in this weakness there is accomplished his lifting up, confirmed by the power of the Resurrection, then this means that the weaknesses of all human sufferings are capable of being infused with the same power of God manifested in Christ's Cross. In such a concept, to suffer means to become particularly susceptible, particularly open to the working of the salvific powers of God, offered to humanity in Christ.

In him God has confirmed his desire to act especially through suffering, which is man's weakness and emptying of self, and he wishes to make his power known precisely in this weakness and emptying of self. This also explains the exhortation in the First Letter of Peter: "Yet if one suffers as a Christian, let him not be ashamed, but under that name let him glorify God" (4:16). In the Letter to the Romans, the apostle Paul deals still more fully with the theme of this "birth of power in weakness," this spiritual tempering of man in the midst of trials and tribulations, which is the particular vocation of those who share in Christ's sufferings.

> More than that, we rejoice in our sufferings, knowing that suffering produces endurance, and endurance produces character, and character produces hope, and hope does not disappoint us, because God's love has been poured into our hearts through the Holy Spirit which has been given to us (Rom 5:3-5).

Suffering as it were contains a special call to the virtue which man must exercise on his own part. And this is the virtue of perseverance in bearing whatever disturbs and causes harm. In doing this, the individual unleashes hope, which maintains in him the conviction that suffering will not get the better of him, that it will not deprive him of his dignity as a human being, a dignity linked to awareness of the meaning of life.

And indeed this meaning makes itself known together with the working of God's love, which is the supreme gift of the Holy Spirit. The more he shares in this love, man rediscovers himself more and more fully in suffering: he rediscovers the "soul" which he thought he had "lost" because of suffering. (*SD*, 23)

- *Return to the words and phrases to which you are most drawn by the Lord. Ponder them reflectively.*
- *Pray from your heart, conversing with the Father, Jesus, the Holy Spirit, and/or Mary.*
- *Pause and receive from God in some time of silent prayer.*

Resolutions for Forming a Life of Marian Consecration

In Jesus' passion and death he shows us the depths of God's love, but also reveals the redemptive meaning of our own sufferings. We are never alone in our suffering. Through a new life of Marian consecration, we benefit from the companionship of Mary. Blessed John Paul II explains:

> The divine Redeemer wishes to penetrate the soul of every sufferer through the heart of His holy Mother, the first and the most exalted of all the redeemed. As though by a continuation of that motherhood which by the power of the Holy Spirit had given him life, the dying Christ conferred upon the ever Virgin Mary a new kind of motherhood — spiritual and universal — toward all human beings, so that every individual, during the pilgrimage of faith, might remain, together with her, closely united to him unto the cross, and so that every form of suffering, given fresh life by the power of this cross, should become no longer the weakness of man but the power of God. (*SD*, 26)

Suggested Resolutions for Today

- *Take a moment to speak to Mary about the significant sufferings in your own life. Allow her to direct you to the consoling love of Christ.*

- *Resolve to form a life of Marian consecration by which you unite your sufferings, big and small, to those of Jesus and Mary.*

- *Sometime today, pray the Rosary.*

Close Your Time of Prayer

With joyful anticipation of your approaching consecration, pray the Prayer to Jesus and the Holy Spirit for the Third Week.

DAY 33

The Resurrection

Begin Your Prayer

Pray the Angelus as an act of presence: Consider the Father's loving gaze upon you, Jesus becoming present to you in Mary, and the Holy Spirit overshadowing you.

Pray for the Light of the Holy Spirit: Pray the Litany of the Holy Spirit with a sense of the Holy Spirit gently penetrating ever deeper into your heart with each invocation.

Form your desire: To come to a fuller knowledge of Jesus and his tremendous love for you so that you may choose him, follow him, adore him, and serve him more fully in your life.

Contemplation

Read slowly and reflectively from Scripture:

Now on the first day of the week Mary Mag'dalene came to the tomb early, while it was still dark, and saw that the stone had been taken away from the tomb. So she ran, and went to Simon Peter and the other disciple, the one whom Jesus loved, and said to them, "They have taken the Lord out of the tomb, and we do not know where they have laid him." Peter then came out with the other disciple, and they went toward the tomb. They both ran, but the other disciple outran Peter and reached the tomb first; and stooping to look in, he saw the linen cloths lying there, but he did not go in. Then Simon Peter came, following him, and went into the tomb; he saw the linen cloths lying, and the napkin, which had been on his head, not lying with the linen cloths but rolled up in a place by itself. Then the other disciple, who reached the tomb first, also went in, and he saw and believed; for as yet they did not know the scripture, that he must rise from the dead. Then the disciples went back to their homes.

But Mary stood weeping outside the tomb, and as she wept she stooped to look into the tomb; and she saw two angels in white, sitting where the body of Jesus had lain, one at the head and one at the feet. They said to her, "Woman, why are you weeping?" She said to them, "Because they have taken away my Lord, and I do not know where they have laid him." Saying this, she turned round and saw Jesus standing, but she did not know that it was Jesus.

Jesus said to her, "Woman, why are you weeping? Whom do you seek?" Supposing him to be the gardener, she said to him, "Sir, if you have carried him away, tell me where you have laid him, and I will take him away." Jesus said to her, "Mary." She turned and said to him in Hebrew, "Rab-bo'ni!" (which means Teacher). Jesus said to her, "Do not hold me, for I have not yet ascended to the Father; but go to my brethren and say to them, I am ascending to my Father and your Father, to my God and your God." Mary Mag'dalene went and said to the disciples, "I have seen the Lord"; and she told them that he had said these things to her. (Jn 20:1-18)

From Blessed John Paul II:

The final destination of Christ's journey through life is not the darkness of the tomb, but the shining heaven of the Resurrection. Christian faith is based on this mystery, as the Catechism of the Catholic Church reminds us: "The Resurrection of Jesus is the crowning truth of our faith in Christ, a faith believed and lived as the central truth by the first Christian community; handed on as fundamental by Tradition; established by the documents of the New Testament; and preached as an essential part of the paschal mystery along with the cross" (CCC, n. 638). . . .

[In] the apparition which takes place in a Jerusalem still bathed in the pale light of dawn: a woman, Mary Magdalene, and a man meet in a cemetery. At first the woman does not recognize the man who has approached her: yet he is that Jesus of Nazareth whom she had listened to and who had changed her life. To recognize him she needs another source of knowledge than reason and the senses. It is the way of faith which is opened to her when she hears herself called by name. (*Gen. Aud.*, May 10, 2000)

- *Return to the words and phrases to which you are most drawn by the Lord. Ponder them reflectively.*

- *Pray from your heart, conversing with the Father, Jesus, the Holy Spirit, and/or Mary.*

- *Pause and receive from God in some time of silent prayer.*

Resolutions for Forming a Life of Marian Consecration

We have reached the final day of preparation for Marian consecration. Throughout the last thirty-three days, we have looked at various characteristics, effects, and attributes of what it means to live a life transformed by Marian consecration. Tomorrow is the day to make the consecration; however, we strive to live out this consecration for the rest of our lives. We do not have to be perfect, but only continue to trust in Mary, and be generous. Jesus will lead us by his grace and advance us as we continue to practice our devotion to Mary in all its interior and exterior forms. Of our entrustment, Blessed John Paul II says:

This filial relationship, this self-entrusting of a child to its mother, not only has its beginning in Christ but can also be said to be definitively directed toward him. Mary can be said to continue to say to each individual the words which she spoke at Cana in Galilee: "Do whatever he tells you." For he, Christ, is the one Mediator between God and mankind; he is "the way, and the truth, and the life" (Jn 14:6); it is he whom the Father has given to the world, so that man "should not perish but have eternal life" (Jn 3:16).

The Virgin of Nazareth became the first "witness" of this saving love of the Father, and she also wishes to remain its humble handmaid always and everywhere. For every Christian, for every human being, Mary is the one who first "believed," and precisely with her faith as Spouse and Mother she wishes to act upon all those who entrust themselves to her as her children. And it is well known that the more her children persevere and progress in this attitude, the nearer Mary leads them to the "unsearchable riches of Christ"(Eph 3:8).

And to the same degree they recognize more and more clearly the dignity of man in all its fullness and the definitive meaning of his vocation, for "Christ ... fully reveals man to man himself" (*GS*, 22). (*RM*, 46)

Suggested Resolutions for Today

- *Prepare to make your consecration tomorrow.*
- *Sometime today, pray the Rosary.*

Close Your Time of Prayer

With joyful anticipation of your approaching consecration, pray the Prayer to Jesus and the Holy Spirit for the Third Week.

DAY OF CONSECRATION

You have completed the thirty-three days of preparation and today is the day of consecration. As planned, it falls on a feast day. Here are some components of this day and for the new life that follows.

- **The Sacrament of Reconciliation:** Plan to receive the Sacrament of Reconciliation today. If unable to arrange confession this day, receive it on a day shortly before or soon after.

- **The Eucharist:** Attend Mass and receive holy Communion. You may wish to prepare for Mass by praying with the readings, using the same method that you did in the contemplation each day of the preparation.

- **The Act of Consecration:** Form the intention of giving yourself to Jesus Christ though Mary. You will pray the formal Act of Consecration sometime after receiving Communion. You may choose to write it out by hand, recite it out loud, and sign and date it.

- **A Tribute of Love to Mary:** Saint Louis de Montfort recommends making a tribute of love to Mary today. The tribute can take many different forms, such as giving alms, lighting a candle, placing flowers before an image of Mary, a fast, or an act of charity. Saint Louis indicates that this act of love should be given according to our own fervor and discretion, saying, "If they had but a pin to give in homage, and gave it with a good heart, it would be enough for Jesus, who looks only at the good will" (*TD*, 232).

- **An External Sign of Devotion:** While optional and not essential, Saint Louis recommends wearing an external sign and reminder of your consecration in the form of little chains around your wrist (symbolic of holy slavery). You may wear a Marian medal or scapular in lieu of the little chains, if you prefer.

- **The Rosary:** In order to help maintain a life of consecration, Saint Louis de Montfort encourages the ongoing and daily practice of some Marian devotions. Preeminent is the Rosary. Strive to pray the Rosary each day, even if you are only able to pray one decade.

- **A New Life of Consecration:** The consecration isn't finished on the day it is prayed; it's only just beginning. Now it is time to live out the consecration on a daily basis. Continue to foster the interior practices of remaining in communion with Jesus and Mary. Deepen your sense of Mary's presence with you, and give all that you are to Jesus through her.

- **Renewal of Consecration:** Once a year or more you should renew your consecration. It is especially meaningful to renew it annually on the same Marian feast day. The preparation for renewal may employ the entire thirty-three-day cycle or simply the three weeks on knowledge of self, Mary, and Jesus. Saint Louis de Montfort also recommends a monthly or even a daily renewal through a brief recollection of the consecration and recommitment with these few words: "I am yours and all I have is yours, O most loving Jesus, through Mary, your most holy Mother" (*TD*, 233).

Or you may prefer the words Blessed John Paul II used that are derived from a suggested renewal of consecration in preparation for receiving holy Communion: "I am totally yours, and all that I have is yours. I take you for my all. O Mary, give me your heart" (*TD*, 266).

ACT OF CONSECRATION

Blessed Mary, Ever-Virgin Mother of Jesus, Faithful Daughter of God the Father, and Spouse of the Holy Spirit: I, _____, a poor sinner, renew and ratify the vows of my baptism. I renounce forever Satan, his works, and his empty promises. I consecrate and give myself entirely to Jesus Christ. I choose to take up my cross and follow him all the days of my life, and to be more faithful to him than I have ever been before. In the presence of all the angels and saints I choose you this day as my Mother and take you into my own heart. I entrust all that I am to you and resolve to honor and love you this day and every day for the rest of my life. O Mary, you have already opened your heart to me! Accept now the gift of my heart, the offering of all that I am to you. Lead me to Jesus that through you I may belong to him, with you I may adore him, in you I may be in communion with him and the Blessed Trinity, and by you I may become so perfectly his disciple so as to glorify him on earth and be led to his glory in Heaven. Amen.

Sign your name here.

Date

About the Author

Fr. Brian McMaster is Director of Vocations and Seminarians for the Diocese of Austin, Texas. He completed seminary at the Pontifical College Josephinum and has an Master of Art in Christian Spirituality from Creighton University. Ordained in 2001, Fr. McMaster has served in numerous assignments including campus ministry at Texas A&M University. He is an adjunct faculty member of the Institute for Priestly Formation. Fr. McMaster is founder and moderator of *Cor Jesu*, an association of diocesan priests devoted to the Heart of Jesus and dedicated to priestly fraternity and the New Evangelization.